TRAVEL SCRAPBOOKS

MEMORY MAKERS BOOKS

contents
travel scrapbooks

62

40

22

complete index

Turn to page 4 for a complete index of ideas in this book! ➤

Executive Editor Deborah Mock

Art Director Mark Lewis

Associate Editor Darlene D'Agostino

Craft Editor Kari Hansen-Daffin

Departments Editor Trisha McCarty-Luedke

Editorial Assistant Sarah Kelly

Senior Graphic Designer Dawn Knutson

Photographer Ken Trujillo

Idea Editor Shawna Rendon

Idea Coordinator Lynda Meisner

Editorial Support Dena Twinem

Contributors

Contributing Writers Heather Eades, Brandi Ginn

Contributing Artist Trudy Sigurdson

Contributing Designers Sarah Daniels, Jeff Norgord, Karen Roehl, Melanie Warner

Contributing Photographers Lizzy Creazzo, Brenda Martinez, Jennifer Reeves

2005 Memory Makers Masters Jessie Baldwin, Jenn Brookover, Christine Brown, Sheila Doherty, Jodi Heinen, Jeniece Higgins, Nic Howard, Julie Johnson, Shannon Taylor, Samantha Walker

F+W Publications, Inc.

Chairman William F. Reilly

President Stephen J. Kent

Executive Vice President & CFO Mark F. Arnett

F+W Publications, Inc. Magazine Division

President William R. Reed

Vice President Consumer Marketing Susan Dubois

Director of Business Planning & Analysis Matt Friedersdorf

Publication Production Manager Vicki Whitford

Special Thanks

We would like to thank all contributors to this book, including those participants whose pages we requested but were not able to feature because of space limitations. We appreciate your willingness to share your ideas—you are what makes this magazine unique.

The material in this book appeared in the previously published Volume 10, No. 52 issue of *Memory Makers*, a division of F+W Publications, Inc., and appears here by permission of the contributors.

Published by Memory Makers Books, an imprint of F+W Publications, Inc.
12365 Huron Street, Suite 500, Denver, CO 80234
Phone 1-800-254-9124

First edition. Printed in the United States of America.

09 08 07 06 05   5 4   3   2   1

A catalog record for this book is available from the Library of Congress
at <http://catalog.loc.gov>.

ISBN 1-892127-70-9

Distributed in Canada by Fraser Direct
100 Armstrong Avenue
Georgetown, ON, Canada L7G 5S4
Tel: (905) 877-4411

Distributed in the U.K. and Europe by David & Charles
Brunel House, Newton Abbot, Devon,
TQ12 4PU, England
Tel: (+44) 1626 323200, Fax: (+44) 1626 323319
Email: mail@davidandcharles.co.uk

Distributed in Australia by Capricorn Link
P.O. Box 704, S. Windsor, NSW 2756 Australia
Tel: (02) 4577-3555

Memory Makers Books is the home of *Memory Makers*, the scrapbook magazine dedicated to educating and inspiring scrapbookers. *Memory Makers* features the ideas and stories of our readers around the world—people who believe in keeping scrapbooks and the tradition of the family photo historian alive. *Memory Makers* is committed to providing ideas and inspiration for this worldwide community of scrapbookers. To subscribe, or for more information, call 1-800-366-6465.

Visit us on the Internet at www.memorymakersmagazine.com.

book index

an index of scrapbook page ideas, products and techniques featured in this book

Journaling On The Road, p. 30

The Traveling Scrapbooker, p. 18

featured scrapbookers

Meet the scrapbookers whose ideas are featured in this book. Each of these contributors receives a gift box containing scrapbook supplies generously donated by leading scrapbook-product manufacturers.

Alabama
Vanessa Hudson – Mt. Olive

California
Hilary Erickson – Santa Clara
Pamela James – Ventura
J. J. Killins – Redondo Beach
Deborah Liu – Santa Clara
Michele Rank – Cerritos
Stacy Yoder – Yucaipa

Colorado
Terri Bradford – Henderson
Sheryl Highsmith – Fort Collins
Kelli Noto – Centennial
Michelle Pendleton
– Colorado Springs
Tricia Rubens – Castle Rock
Andrea Vetten-Marley – Aurora
Cherie Ward – Colorado Springs

Georgia
Danielle Thompson – Tucker

Idaho
ℳ Sheila Doherty – Coeur d'Alene
Becky Thompson – Fruitland

Illinois
ℳ Jeniece Higgins – Lake Forest
Tracey Lee – Dwight
Lynne Rigazzio-Mau – Channahon

Indiana
Amy Alvis – Indianapolis
Katy Jurasevich – Crown Point
Denise Tucker – Versailles

Iowa
Lori Ann Lewis – Des Moines

Louisiana
Madeline Fox – River Ridge

Michigan
Jennifer Bourgeault
– Macomb Township
Michelle Mueller – Albion

Minnesota
Laurel Gervitz – Maple Grove
Vicki Harvey – Champlin
ℳ Jodi Heinen – Sartell
Sandra Stephens – Woodbury

Mississippi
Valerie Barton – Flowood

Montana
Becky Fleck – Columbus

Nevada
ℳ Jessie Baldwin – Las Vegas

New York
Leah Blanco Williams – Rochester
Joanne MacIntyre – Medford

North Carolina
Joanna Bolick – Fletcher

Ohio
Amanda Goodwin – Munroe Falls
Barb Hogan – Cincinnati

Oklahoma
Rosemary Waits – Mustang

Pennsylvania
Susan Weinroth – Philadelphia

South Carolina
Patti Milazzo – Lexington

Tennessee
Donette Buxton – Nashville
Danielle Layton – Clarksville
Bay Loftis – Philadelphia
Cindy Smith – Knoxville

Texas
ℳ Jenn Brookover – San Antonio
ℳ Julie Johnson – Seabrook
Donna Pittard – Kingwood
Pam Sivage – Georgetown
Melissa Smith
– North Richland Hills
Kara Wylie – Frisco

Utah
Heidi Dillon – Salt Lake City

Washington
ℳ Samantha Walker – Battle Ground

Wisconsin
Heidi Schueller – Waukesha

International

Australia
Colleen Macdonald – Winthrop

Canada
Janice Carson – Hamilton, Ontario
Mary MacAskill – Calgary, Alberta
Shelley McLennan
– St. Catharines, Ontario
Elma Regnerus – Grimsby, Ontario
Yolanda Robinson
– Kelowna, British Columbia
Trudy Sigurdson
– Victoria, British Columbia
Sharon Whitehead
– Vernon, British Columbia

Ireland
Emma Finlay – Dublin

New Zealand
ℳ Nic Howard
– Pukekohe, South Auckland

South Africa
Meryl Bartho – Pinetown, KwaZulu

ℳ This logo denotes a current Memory Makers Master.

send us your ideas | featured scrapbookers

Common Threads, p. 53

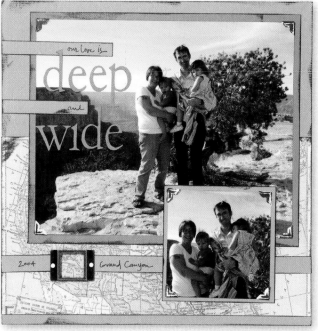

Reader Idea Gallery, p. 71

scraphappenings

the latest travel tools, supplies, ideas and news for the avid scrapbooker

See page 8 for this fun page

Traveler's Paradise

Journey through a world of travel-themed scrapbooking products

It seems that there are almost more travel-themed scrapbooking products available than world cultures. Picking the perfect products to document your journey is a journey in itself. Relive your vacation by lingering on location-specific accessories. In this special "Scraphappenings" section, we've rounded up the most exciting travel products available and organized them according to destination. Have a nice trip...to your local scrapbook store or favorite online store to look for these products and more to adorn your travel scrapbook pages.

American Traditional Designs is one of many companies creating products that lend a well-traveled look to vacation memories. Antiqued maps, archaic compasses and weathered travel accessories join distressed clips, frames, stamps and stickers for a sense of the rare and historic. Colleen Rundgren for American Traditional Designs created the passport mini album shown left and below. The album cover is made from cut paper, which Colleen embossed to look like an actual passport. Inside, the album contains postcardlike pages with photos and journaling that pull out of pocket pages. These pages also were adorned with stamped images, distressed with ink and lavished in ephemera.

supplies: Patterned papers, charms, stickers, globe template, stencil, brads, rub-ons (American Traditional) • Ephemera (Provo Craft) • Label holder (Making Memories) • Letter brad (Colorbök) • Stamps (Stampin' Up, Stampabilities) • File folders (DMD) • Label maker (Dymo) • Zig photo-tinting markers (EK Success)

vintage style

If you are looking for classic, travel-themed products, check out Me & My Big Ideas (MAMBI) Scrappychic product line. Suzy Plantamura for MAMBI created the tag above using papers, stickers and ephemera from the Scrappychic Vintage Collection. She also used Vintage Threads woven labels and Inspirational Sayings rub-ons.

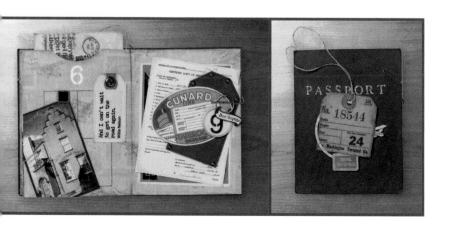

road trip

From squealing tire-track to license-plate stickers and accents, the look and feel of the open road can be found at Sticker Studio (**stickerstudio .com**). The Road Trip collection combines highly textured highway signs, embossed patterned papers for extra dimension and more for a fast and freewheeling look. 99 cents – $4.99

ART: NANCY BURKE FOR STICKER STUDIO

ART: TRUDY SIGURDSON (MASTERS '03)

retro disney

To add a softer, more subdued tone to those family-focused adventures, Sandylion (**sandylion.com**) has revived classic Disney stickers and patterned papers with retro appeal. Enjoy the classic characters on each clear mylar sticker sheet and vintage patterned-paper design. 50 cents – $2

state tags

Handmade highlights from all 50 states are available on Travel Tags from Reminisce (**designsbyreminisce.com**). These highly textural accents lend depth and location-specific detail to any vacation in the nation. Each classic design incorporates fibers and metal accents for a nostalgic, sophisticated look. $5 per tag.

touristy treats

Picture this: Your Dad in his Hawaiian-print shirt, fanny-pack and a camera draped around his neck. Now, picture this: Stamps to highlight his touristy tendencies. Rubber Baby Buggy Bumpers (rubberbaby.com) travel stamps feature proverbial tourists Mr. and Mrs. Bon Voyage as well as mobile homes and well-loved luggage. All are images that capture the heart and soul of traveling across America. Perfect for cross-country travel pages, these unique and whimsical images capture the fun of being a foreigner in your own country.
$6 – $14

ART: MELANY SIMPSON FOR QUICKUTZ

city-slicker dies

Quickutz (quickutz.com) Cityscape die set makes documenting a trip to any major city a cinch. Overlap cut shapes of skyscrapers, high-rises and lofts to re-create any metropolitan adventure. Using the die set with the Quickutz Hand Tool, simply slide dies in, press and pop out city shapes. $31.99 per set

ART: STACEY HACKETT FOR FLAIR DESIGNS

flair designs

Make your scrapbook pages a day at the beach with colors, quotes and a splash of cool. Flair Designs (**flairdesignsinc.com**) Summer Fun Collection consists of vibrant patterned papers, playful cardstock stickers and vellum sheets with surfer words and summer-inspired quotes. Use them to capture the memories of sand and sea.
60 cents – $3.50

tropical treasures

Bright colors that reflect the warmth of the sun and the brilliant cool of the ocean bring the essence of sitting seaside home to refresh your vacation memories. Sandylion's (**sandylion.com**) Tropics collection features paper selections in cheerful tone-on-tone patterns using juicy splashes of saturated color. These provide the perfect backdrop for energetic coordinating accent and letter stickers. For warm-weather travel memories, Hawaiian dream getaways, or for simply highlighting those days spent at the beach, these hand-painted designs of papers, stickers, letters and icons will set a tone of invigorating joy and refreshing fun to your page.
40 cents – $6.99

ART: SHEILA DOHERTY (MASTERS '05)

go west studios

Go West Studios (**goweststudios.com**) reveals its new Beach and Travel Line. The Acrylic Chunky and Funky Word Tag Set features beach-themed words on tags. Just as beachy are the Acrylic Word Buckle Set, which are ribbon accents, and Acrylic Frames. Also available are Wood Shell frames, Acrylic and Wood Word Trios, Colored Acrylic Word Chimes and Acrylic and Metal Words. $2.29 – $8.49

bright rub-ons

Summer Expressionz rub-ons from Junkitz (**junkitz.com**) turn up the heat on any beach motif with carefree sentiments in tropical tones. Each hand-lettered, acid-free phrase can be applied to papers, photos, fabric, metal, glass and plastic. These highly versatile keynotes of summer coordinate with Junkitz embellishments and each word can be cut apart to use the letters separately. $3.99 per sheet

soft spoken labels

With beachcomber Soft Spoken embellishments from Me & My Big Ideas (**meand mybigideas.com**), thoughts of paradise can highlight oceanfront layouts. Each unique dimensional accent is handcrafted in textures and tones from the soul of the surf. Available in packages of four, these delights can be attached easily to most surfaces with their self-adhesive backings. Shimmer, shine, stitching and twine are all a part of these textural treasures. $4 per pack

ART: WENDY MALICHIO FOR PAPER HOUSE PRODUCTIONS

Europe by train has been a long time dream of ours. We had gone on a small trip from Zurich to St. Anton in Austria for our honeymoon, but this time we were going to take the night train through Europe. When thinking of trains and Europe, I always think of how James Bond travels in style. This is my yardstick for train travel, so when we went on this trip it was extra exiting to get our very own compartment in the train wagon. We just sat there and really enjoyed our trip. The views were magnificent and it was very nice to travel by train. I remembered the famous words by Hans Christian Andersen, the Danish writer: to travel is to live. How true! September 23, 2004

masterpiece products

Paper House Productions (**paperhousepro ductions.com**) Impressions line brings the heart and art of Europe to scrapbook pages with the timeless paintings of the French Impressionist painters. For travels abroad, the Impressions collection of papers and accents showcases the everyday scenes of Paris, London, Tuscany and more, utilizing flickering brush strokes of color and light from Master artists such as van Gogh, Cézanne, Monet and Renoir. 75 cents – $1.99

elegant titles

For something simple and dramatic, try a laser-cut from Sarah Heidt Photo Craft (sarahheidtphotocraft.com). These flowing titles are set in the Scriptina font and are cut from Bazzill Basics paper. Playful photo tile embel-lishments, such as the double-decker bus shown below, are the thickness of a penny and are made from acid-free plastic. 80 cents – $5

ART: SHEILA DOHERTY (MASTERS '05)

label stamps

If you've traveled across Europe, label stamps from ERA Graphics (**eragraphics .com**) will help you title journaling blocks, travel journals or cre-ate borders for pages showing several locales. Each stamp offers rich letters and images with the look of a woodcut print. The label stamps come on a sheet and are unmounted, either 19 or 23 label stamps per sheet. $20 per sheet; 2 for $35

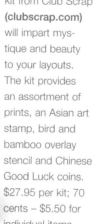

asian accents

The Asian Artisan kit from Club Scrap (**clubscrap.com**) will impart mystique and beauty to your layouts. The kit provides an assortment of prints, an Asian art stamp, bird and bamboo overlay stencil and Chinese Good Luck coins. $27.95 per kit; 70 cents – $5.50 for individual items

parisian flair

Capturing the majestic grandeur of French cathedrals in timeless tones and textures, Bisous (**bisous. biz**) provides an assortment of papers and cutouts that transfer Parisian beauty to correlating scrapbook pages. Bisous also offers a Paris Travel Scrapbooking and Cardmaking Kit. 70 cents – $1.98; $9.50 for the kit

Creating Vacation Scrapbook Pages

Need more inspiration for your travel albums? Look no further than this Memory Makers book. Whether you've got your sights set on a new travel destination or are looking to scrapbook your past adventures, this resource will ensure

that the "getting there" of the page-creating process is half the fun. Inside you'll discover hundreds of page ideas that cover everything from shore-side escapes to eye-opening domestic and international travels. Also included is a helpful don't-leave-home-without-it list of essentials for the traveling scrapbooker, tips for postcard-perfect vacation photos and more. On sale now.

scrapyourtrip.com

Looking for the perfect page embellishment for your travel album? Check out Scrapyourtrip.com. This Web site carries more than 3,000 papers, stickers and die cuts for all 50 states, 80-plus countries, Disney and more. Plus, if you are looking for a hard-to-find item, company representatives will help locate it for you.

Free clip art!

Visit pccrafter.com/ mmm for a special collection of free travel and vacation clip art courtesy of pcCrafter. If you register with pcCrafter, the company will give you $10 worth of free clip art! Travel images include suitcases, airplanes and more.

the traveling
scrapbooker

3 foolproof plans for taking scrapbooking on the road

by Darlene D'Agostino

Scrapbooking while traveling—is that laughable? Perhaps for some, but trust us, it can be done. We'll prove it!

This article details three tried-and-true blueprints for scrapbooking on the road. Meet four scrapbookers who love to save the memories as they make them. Each has her own method, but the result is the same: outstanding travel albums ready (or near ready) the moment she steps off the plane or unpacks the car.

The first plan focuses on the "road tripper." She explains how to scrapbook with paper, scissors and glue in the car and at the pool and the hotel.

The second scrapbooker, the "traditional collector," provides detailed tips on how to methodically collect memorabilia and other scrapbook treasures and complete journaling while traveling. Travel albums will come together easily once you arrive home.

Finally, head into the modern age with two "digital explorers." With their trusty laptops, they generate digital scrapbook pages before arriving home.

Model your own travel scrapbooking after one of the plans or glean tips from all three to create a new method.

the road tripper

Complete a travel album before arriving home from your trip with the scrapbooking program recommended by MaryJo Regier, Memory Makers Books Senior Editor. MaryJo is a mother of four and road-trip queen. Her mantra: preplan, pack light and stay organized.

the traditional collector

Kelli Noto (Masters '03) offers her hunter-gatherer approach for the traveling scrapbooker. Kelli scouts out information-packed brochures and nostalgia-inducing mementos to invigorate her scrapbook pages with detail once she arrives home.

the digital explorers

Scrapbookers Meryl Bartho of Pinetown, KwaZulu Natal, South Africa, and Susan Foraker of Austin, Texas, blaze the technology trail to offer a complete method for digital scrapbooking on the road. Use your digital camera, laptop and software to complete pages on the go.

MaryJo Regier

Preplan, pack light and stay organized, says MaryJo. Adopt these three guidelines and scrapbooking on the road will be a smooth ride. Preplanning a trip-in-progress album also will psych you up for your trip.

the lowdown
The greatest reward of this method: "Coming home with a completed album while the memory is still fresh," MaryJo says. It's also a fun family activity that captures great moments as they happen. Scrapbook on the road, and you won't ever forget the little things that made a trip great.

what to pack
Small cutting mat, craft knife, metal ruler, scissors, small paper trimmer, adhesives, two or three pens and one or two simple design tools such as a corner rounder and/or decorative scissors—protect these items from theft and the elements.

special considerations
Don't alienate your family or let scrapbooking interfere with the fun, MaryJo says. Her family is very good about telling her when enough is enough.

photos
Part of MaryJo's preplanning includes scouring travel magazines and brochures for photo ops. "I'll pre-order destination brochures also so I'll know what I'm up against shot-wise," she says. "Since I've thought through the 'big' shots, my mind is free to focus on the fun candid photos."

journaling
Record and record often—that way you won't forget. MaryJo jots notes throughout the day, and at the end of the day, she records the day's events in chronological order. She transfers the notes into the album while riding in the car. "I've learned to love bumpy, road-weary penmanship," she says. "It adds character to the album." She likes to include details about the weather, the route taken, funny things her family says and does, her impressions of the day, prices, food choices, likes and dislikes and anything she and her family have learned.

From Las Vegas to San Diego

Scrapbooking on the road gives MaryJo something to do during downtime, whether it occurs during car rides, at the pool, late at night or while her boys (her husband and four sons) trek off to do "guy things," she says. For this album, MaryJo developed her film every few days at one-hour photo finishers and printed enlargements at photo kiosks. To ensure a cohesive look, she used a corner rounder on all of the photos. She also kept the album journaling-focused. Each member of her family added his thoughts on a journaling sticker on the last page (shown right). The blank sticker represents her youngest son, Hunter, who did not know how to write at the time. To create a similar album, limit yourself to two or three pen colors; use consistent design tools on each page (such as the same corner rounder) and choose accents that are similar in style (stickers, die cuts, etc.).

supplies: 8 x 8" album (Kolo) • Blue, black papers • Corner rounder • Blue, black pens • Colored pencils • Deckle scissors

When scrapbooking on the road, MaryJo's goal is saving the memories. "I focus on my journaling, not amazing page design," she says. "These albums are really about the memories, not my creative expression." She recommends working with a smaller album format such as 8 x 8". It's easier to work with, but keep in mind it most likely will not fit all of your photos.

photo *processing*

Print your own or visit a local photo finisher.

portable mini printers Compact mini printers the size of a medium handbag and that also plug into a car cigarette lighter will print your 4 x 6" photos on the go. Both the Epson PictureMate and Hewlett-Packard Photosmart 245 print high-quality photos without the need of a computer.

photo finisher Drop off your finished rolls of film to a one-hour film developer. Or if you have two memory cards for your digital camera, you can drop off the full card to a developer while you fill up the second. Ask the developer to burn the photos to a disk for a backup and to share with friends and family. Or, hit up a photo-printing kiosk and print your own. Be sure to delete unwanted shots before you use it. Fuji, Kodak, Sony and Polaroid have kiosks. Visit their Web sites for locations and special offers.

scrapbooking *on the fly*

Here are MaryJo's top 5 tips for success:

preplan Pick your page size. Research the destination, (find maps and brochures online; visitors centers will send them for free). Use them to inspire journaling and to create themed accents. Choose the color scheme and raid your supplies for travel product. Find the local scrapbook store where you are vacationing for location-specific accents.

make page kits Once you have destination research materials, pre-assemble page kits with paper and a few accents such as stickers (remember, you can buy accents on the road or spruce up the album once you are home).

pack lightly Avoid the temptation to take a big, wheeled tote. MaryJo likes the Crop-In-Style Paper Sticker Binder, inside of which she stores page kits that she completes before the trip.

stay organized Toss the refuse—paper scraps and cropping remnants make a mess on the road. Get a tote to accommodate both supplies and finished art. Maintain your system after shopping for accents or getting photos developed.

journal immediately Once photos are developed, journal the date, the details and potential page ideas.

the traditional collector: Kelli Noto

This scrapbooking-on-the-road method is the least intrusive on your family time. It simply requires the presence of mind to snag brochures, collect small items such as matchbooks, buy picture-perfect postcards and journal.

the lowdown
Grab information-packed brochures and mementos to scrapbook once home. This allows Kelli to have fun with her family because she is not so concerned with recording every single detail. She journals to keep track of the memories and takes simple snapshots.

what to pack
Not much—Kelli travels armed with a notebook in which she journals. She stows mementos in her suitcase or, if driving, a seat pocket. Accordion folders, envelopes or plastic bags also are great for organizing mementos.

photos
Although she is a professional photographer, Kelli avoids bringing her best equipment with her as her goal is not "to replicate picture-perfect postcards," she says. She focuses on her family, taking snapshots of them with famous landmarks acting as magnificent backdrops.

journaling
While Kelli does include factual information, she tends to focus on impressions. "Our family has a vacation tradition of summing up the day's events with a Haiku poem, and I write these little musings in the notebook," she says. She also gives the notebook to her boys to sketch in or journal.

design inspiration
Kelli looks to brochures for design inspiration. "I figure that a professional team of graphic designers has already chosen colors and fonts to evoke the mood of a destination—they are a good source of design inspiration," she says.

National Parks Tour

Kelli eloquently sums up her method: "If you want to go to Zion National Park to photograph Zion National Park, you leave your children at home, wake up very early in the morning for the best light and lug a heavy tripod and expensive camera with you on every trail. But, if you want to *see* Zion National Park, you bring along those you love, visit the places that call to your heart and take quick snapshots so you can enjoy the time that you have together on vacation. There are photographers who have photographed the park in the best light, with great equipment—buy their postcards."

supplies: Black, terra cotta, green papers • Handmade paper • Transparency • Empire, Empire Minis, Frankie, Frankie Minis, Eliza, Eliza Minis letter dies (Quickutz) • Eyelets, brads (Happy Hammer) • Circle punch • Acrylic paint (Plaid) • National Park brochures (sprayed with de-acidification spray) • Computer fonts

Upon returning home, the pages for Kelli's travel album came together quickly because she didn't reinvent the wheel for each page. She kept a consistent linear page design that she simply varied for each page. She chose three colors and stuck with the scheme. Her font choice is consistent and all the journaling is printed on a transparency. Smaller cropped shots add detailed borders to each page.

more **memorabilia** *tips*

Here are some reader tips on what to collect, where to find it and what to do with it.

what to collect The most popular items to grab are brochures, napkins, matches, fliers, receipts, postcards and ticket stubs. But keep your eye out for the unusual. "My latest favorite is the 'stretched penny,'" says Doris Lemert, owner of Destination Stickers and Stamps. "My daughter loves to flatten and emboss a penny with a souvenir design. These machines are virtually everywhere."

where to find it Visitors centers will be a wealth of mementos, stories and facts. Other places to find interesting tidbits are hotels, truck stops, the foyers of many businesses (free local publications, fliers) and restaurants and pubs (napkins, matches, menus).

what to do with it Consider creating a pocket on one of the inside covers of your album, recommends Emily Tyner of Charlotte, North Carolina. Or, if the items are too bulky, photograph them to include on pages, says Colleen Macdonald of Winthrop, Australia.

To incorporate the brochures into the design, Kelli made a simple pocket for each page into which she slipped the brochures. This consistent pocket treatment adds to the album's unity and also keeps the brochures accessible.

Meryl Bartho & Susan Foraker

Meryl

Susan

Capture vacation memories with the help of a laptop. You have complete creative control without having to worry about scrapbooking supplies.

the lowdown

"This type of scrapbooking allows me to quickly chronicle my life with my family," Susan says. "I can create pages on an airplane and quickly upload them to (a photo-sharing Web site such as) Ofoto or Shutterfly from my hotel room and slip the printed copies into my binder when I get home to share with my children."

what to pack

You will need a laptop computer, a digital camera plus all cords necessary for downloading photos and image-editing, scrapbooking or word-processing software.

special considerations

Take photos at the highest resolution possible, Susan says, because the higher the resolution, the more control you will have when cropping and with special effects. Also, save images to a CD to archive. This frees up space on your hard drive, she says.

photos

Meryl is sure to capture photos of elements that she might like to use as accents, she says, such as birds, botanical images or food.

journaling

Meryl keeps a detailed notebook. In it she writes about what her family has seen, funny memories and route information, which she transfers to her digital layout for journaling. She usually writes while traveling in the car.

design inspirations

Susan relies on scrapbooking magazines which, she notes, fit nicely into a laptop case. Scrapbooking software programs will have templates and digital accents to use. Meryl collects memorabilia such as maps, menus and brochures to scan and use as common accents in her albums.

Namibia Album

When Meryl sets out to create a digital album, she says she first designs a digital kit that consists of backgrounds and accents. For this trip, she kept the backgrounds "earthy and rich" to complement the desert color palette. "I like my album to have a uniform look," Meryl says. For the accents, once home Meryl typically scans mementos from the trip or creates them from photos she takes. The tags in the above layout were created from the price tag of the wall hanging the artisan is holding in the photo.

supplies: Photoshop Creative Suite image-editing software (Adobe) • Digital backgrounds and elements (Meryl's own design, available at digitalscrapbooking.com)

We made an early start from Zambezi River Lodge in Katima and were waved a cheery farewell by the missionaries, for our drive across Caprivi Strip, heading for Popa Falls. It was wonderful to arrive at a campsite in daylight for a change, and especially one so pretty as this one. Although the camping area was very sandy, we had it all to ourselves and it was probably one of the most scenic we had, with a lovely view of the falls - bit of a misnomer though, rapids would be closer to the truth! Another "best" here were the ablutions - attractive, spacious and with piping hot water - wish we could have packed them & taken them along with us......

let's get **digital**

The following is a list of tips to help make life easier for the digital scrapbooker

delete unwanted photos as you go Digital cameras offer ability to instantly view photos and delete unwanted images. This frees up memory on your camera card and saves you time when sifting through dozens of images.

bring an extra memory card This offers the peace of mind of knowing you have an extra camera memory if you need it. Also, as your memory card fills up, it may slow your camera. Having a spare card will allow you to switch out the cards if shots require a fast camera.

burn images to disks If your laptop does not have a CD burner, take the memory card to a photo finisher to have the images burned. This frees up space on both your camera and laptop and backs up your photos. Also, if you are traveling with or visiting family and friends, it makes photo-sharing easy. Simply have an extra CD burned to give away.

Meryl creates all of her own accents. For "Popa Falls" (top left), she created the frames from a photo of the wood from her dining room table. For "Into Namibia" (top right), the items in the pocket are scanned mementos. She created the stamps from flower and tree photos. For "Beautiful Spitzkoppe" (above), the texture of the outer rim of the circle tag is taken from a photo of a wall hanging.

Journaling
on the Road

Relive your travel adventures by capturing the moment with these journaling tools and tips.

by Jennifer Vet

The thrill of the journey lies in the adventure of experiencing new places, meeting new people and seeing the world from a different perspective. As you embark on your next trip, chronicle your experiences while in the midst of your voyage. Record your daily adventures as you live them while they are still fresh in your mind. Before you start packing for your next voyage, take a look at the many options for journaling en route.

Journal Jottings

Romantic souls may prefer jotting their travel log into a journal book. This journaling style is for more prolific writers: more room, more details, more time. Since you will be spending quality time with your journal, pick one that suits your needs and that you will enjoy using. A classic journal allows plenty of room to record details, emotions and accounts. Use creative journaling prompts to inspire you (see p. 45 for ideas). Back home, draw from your journal jottings to express a true sense of place as you scrapbook your photos. The writing can be used in whole or in part throughout a travel album. Revise your writings to fit a layout theme or scan and print journal pages to be used as journaling segments right on a scrapbook page. Small journals might be placed directly onto a layout: tucked into a pocket or protected in a niche. Joanna Bolick (Masters '04) used a clear plastic pocket (see right) to hold a spiral notebook she kept in her backpack while traveling in Australia. Including a journal directly on the page preserves travel memories as well as handwriting.

travels

on the road in Melbourne, Australia 2001

Thanks to Mark's generous bosses, Mark and I had the opportunity to travel together to balmy Melborne, Australia for two weeks in early 2001. While in Australia, we worked at an Ausglass conference (the real reason for our trip) and also enjoyed a week of vacation that included sight-seeing trips, a few tennis matches at the Australian Open, wandering through the many parks of Melbourne, and some unsightly sunburn. During our travels we kept track of our thoughts and experiences in a little journal, so that we would be sure never to forget such an amazing, wonderful, fun-filled journey. 1.21.01-2.2.01

Joanna Bolick (Masters '04) can flip open this pocket-size journal any time and be swept back to Australia by reading her journaling. On her trip, Joanna jotted journaling in the notebook. Upon arrival home, she incorporated the notebook into her page design by tucking it into a plastic pocket.

supplies: Patterned paper (Rusty Pickle) • Black paper • Chipboard alphabet (Li'l Davis) • Diamond Glaze clear gloss medium (Judikins) • Spiral notebook • Plastic pocket • Computer fonts

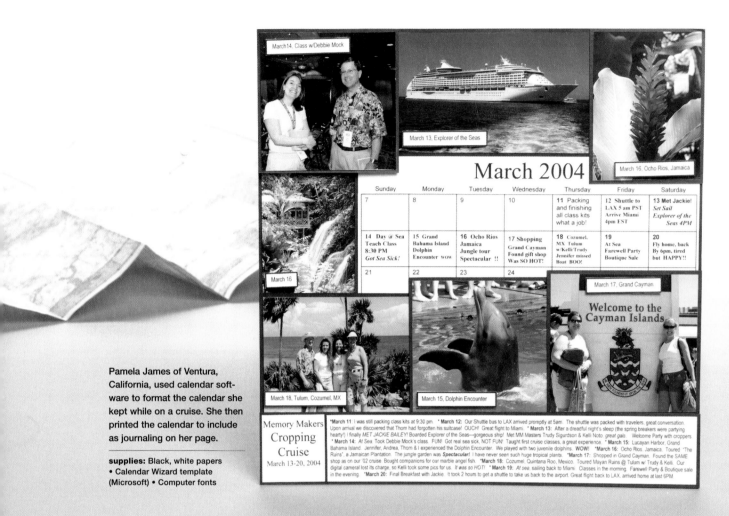

March 14, Class w/Debbie Mock

March 13, Explorer of the Seas

March 16, Ocho Rios, Jamaica

March 2004

Sunday	Monday	Tuesday	Wednesday	Thursday	Friday	Saturday
7	8	9	10	11 Packing and finishing all class kits what a job!	12 Shuttle to LAX 5 am PST Arrive Miami 4pm EST	13 Met Jackie! *Set Sail Explorer of the Seas 4PM*
14 Day @ Sea Teach Class 8:30 PM *Got Sea Sick!*	15 Grand Bahama Island Dolphin Encounter WOW	16 Ocho Rios Jamaica Jungle tour Spectacular !!	17 Shopping Grand Cayman Found gift shop Was SO HOT!	18 Cozumel, MX Tulum w/Kelli/Trudy Jennifer missed Boat BOO!	19 At Sea Farewell Party Boutique Sale	20 Fly home, back By 6pm, tired but HAPPY!!
21	22	23	24			

March 16

March 17, Grand Cayman

Welcome to the Cayman Islands

March 18, Tulum, Cozumel, MX

March 15, Dolphin Encounter

Memory Makers Cropping Cruise
March 13-20, 2004

March 11: I was still packing class kits at 9:30 pm. * **March 12:** Our Shuttle bus to LAX arrived promptly at 5am. The shuttle was packed with travelers; great conversation. Upon arrival we discovered that Thom had forgotten his suitcase! OUCH! Great flight to Miami. * **March 13:** After a dreadful night's sleep (the spring breakers were partying hearty!) I finally MET JACKIE BAILEY! Boarded Explorer of the Seas—gorgeous ship! Met MM Masters Trudy Sigurdson & Kelli Noto: great gals. Welcome Party with croppers. * **March 14:** At Sea. Took Debbie Mock's class. FUN! Got real sea sick, NOT FUN! Taught first cruise classes, a great experience. * **March 15:** Lucayan Harbor, Grand Bahama Island. Jennifer, Andrea, Thom & I experienced the Dolphin Encounter. We played with two juvenile dolphins. WOW! * **March 16:** Ocho Rios, Jamaica. Toured "The Ruins", a Jamaican Plantation. The jungle garden was *Spectacular!* I have never seen such huge tropical plants. * **March 17:** Shopped in Grand Cayman. Found the SAME shop as on our '02 cruise. Bought companions for our marble angel fish. * **March 18:** Cozumel, Quintana Roo, Mexico. Toured Mayan Ruins @ Tulum w/ Trudy & Kelli. Our digital camera lost its charge, so Kelli took some pics for us. It was so HOT! * **March 19:** At sea, sailing back to Miami. Classes in the morning. Farewell Party & Boutique sale in the evening. * **March 20:** Final Breakfast with Jackie. It took 2 hours to get a shuttle to take us back to the airport. Great flight back to LAX, arrived home at last 6PM.

Pamela James of Ventura, California, used calendar software to format the calendar she kept while on a cruise. She then printed the calendar to include as journaling on her page.

supplies: Black, white papers • Calendar Wizard template (Microsoft) • Computer fonts

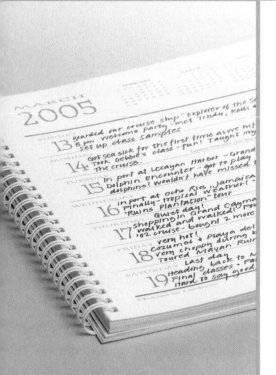

Calendar Comments

Track the bare essentials by journaling into a calendar while you travel. Whether you are a minimalist writer or short on time, a calendar provides a concise space to record each day's adventures plus a few choice particulars. Use your appointment book or a pocket calendar to record short descriptions and basic facts whenever you have a spare moment. For long trips or those with intensive itineraries, this bare-bones account provides a framework to encapsulate the varied aspects of your trip.

At home, your calendar journal becomes a practical tool that can service scrapbook pages in many ways. Let the notes it contains spark expounded journaling now that you have more time, or apply its information directly for a trip synopsis. Pam James of Ventura, California, used calendar software to format the calendar she kept while on a cruise (shown left). This easy-to-use program allowed Pam to customize the calendar grid and then type into each block. When she was ready to create the page shown above, Pam printed out the calendar to include on her page.

Convert your calendar journaling into a linear progression by building a formal timeline or a loose chronological format. Jessie Baldwin (Masters '05) used a calendar to journal in during a Belgium trip. Upon returning home, Jessie created a free-form horizontal chronology from her calendar journaling to provide a trip overview to include on her page (see below).

Laptop Reports

If you travel with a laptop, take advantage of its word processing abilities to keep a journal right on your hard drive. After a day of sightseeing, spend some downtime with your laptop journal and record your recollections of the outing. If you are using a digital camera, this is also a perfect time to download the photos and place them into folders. Journaling straight into a computer allows you to edit your text as you go. Type A personalities will appreciate the efficiency and control laptop journaling entails, both on the road and back at home. When later designing your scrapbook pages, simply edit and format journaling already on your laptop to prepare it for layouts.

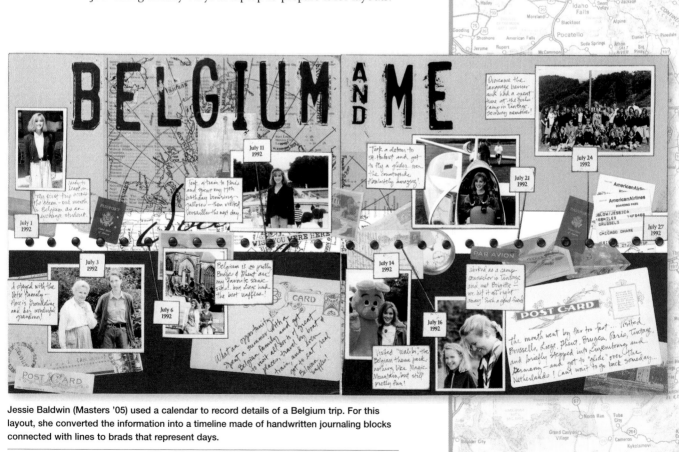

Jessie Baldwin (Masters '05) used a calendar to record details of a Belgium trip. For this layout, she converted the information into a timeline made of handwritten journaling blocks connected with lines to brads that represent days.

supplies: Blue, yellow papers • Printed transparency (Creative Imaginations) • Letter stickers (Mustard Moon) • Travel stickers (Me & My Big Ideas) • Brads • Stamping ink • Renaissance font (twopeasinabucket.com)

E-mail Updates

For most of us, e-mail has become a part of our daily lives, allowing quick and easy communication between family and friends. While traveling, take further advantage of this modern convenience as a practical journaling tool. Use the same trip reports you send via e-mail to your friends as a travel log for your layouts by carbon copying the e-mail to yourself. A growing number of locations will lend you a computer and Internet connection, such as cyber cafes, airports, public libraries and hotels, but be sure to inquire about access fees.

With the journaling already on your computer in an e-mail, it is easy to cut and paste the text into a word processing program. Consider incorporating the structure of e-mail itself on your layouts for a modern twist. On her page "E-Traveler" shown below, Danielle Thompson of Tucker, Georgia, integrated the contemporary format of the e-mail messages she wrote from Italy right into the page design.

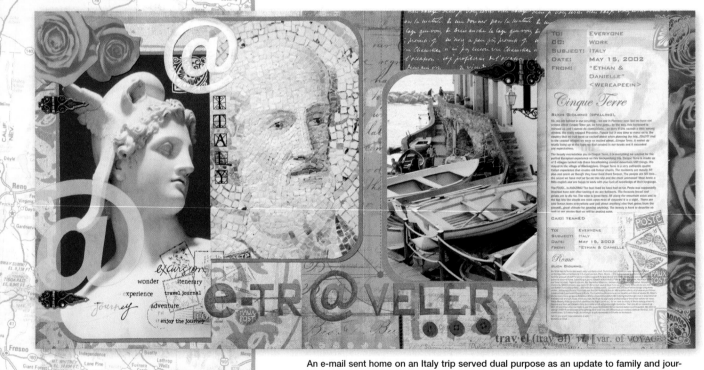

An e-mail sent home on an Italy trip served dual purpose as an update to family and journaling once Danielle Thompson of Tucker, Georgia, returned home. Danielle replicated the e-mail to include it on her page as a journaling block. The e-mail theme is played up with her title—"E-Traveler."

supplies: Gold, red papers • Patterned papers (Basicgrey, 7 Gypsies, Flair, Daisy D's, K & Co.) • Buttons • Metallic rub-ons • Rub-ons (Making Memories, EK Success) • Rubber stamp (Inkadinkado) • Stamping ink • Chalks • Ribbon • Computer fonts

Jonathan and I had the opportunity to do a road trip of a lifetime when we set off to see Kuri, Iwakuni, Miyajima, Hiroshima and Kyoto. Japan is marked with incredible ancient architecture, beautiful gardens, tons of traffic, and countless pedestrians going about their daily business. When we arrived in Miyajima, we were awe struck by the famous tori in the water. It appeared to just float on the surface of the water. Japanese maple were abundant in the palace garden that was home to the tori. As we walked through the streets of this small village, our senses were awakened by the smell of rain, pungent fish markets and rice cooking in the restaurants.

Summer 1997

INSPIRED BEAUTY

While in Japan, Samantha Walker (Masters '05) journaled and sketched scenery into a small sketch book. Inspired by her leaf sketch, Samantha stamped and then cut out the paper leaves. For added dimension, she then folded and creased the leaves.

supplies: Brown shimmer paper (Prism) • Tea Green paper (Bazzill) • Patterned papers (American Traditional, Enchanted Compliments) • Copper, grass papers (Flax) • Plum, brown, sienna papers • Rub-on sentiment (American Traditional) • Brads, date stamp (Making Memories) • Label holder • Photo corners • Red Shimmer paint pen (Krylon) • Stamping ink (Ranger) • Maple leaf stamp, eggplant stamping ink (Stampin' Up) • Pepita MT font (downloaded from the Internet) • Cezanne font (p22.com)

Sketchbook Sentiments

Some of us have an urge to doodle as well as write while on vacation, so pack an unlined artist's sketchbook. They can be found at art supply stores in a variety of sizes and formats. The wide open space of a sketchbook invites imagination and allows creative thinkers generous room for visual notes as they travel. Pair your written journaling with drawings of sights, textures, shapes and motifs observed en route. Note inspiring ideas that develop along the way, such as color schemes and layout compositions, to preserve them for later use when planning scrapbook pages.

After the trip, your sketchbook will not only provide fabulous written accounts of your travels, but numerous visual references. This combination can result in meaningful layouts that capture your journey. Samantha Walker (Masters '05) used a sketchbook throughout her stay in Japan to record her impressions. Once she was home again, Samantha referred to her sketchbook over and over again for design inspiration for her page shown above.

Woodrow loved Fremont Street ~ the old casinos, the street performers, the kiosks of kitschy stuff for sale everywhere. It was all cool to my oh-so-geeky kid.

We saw a rock band with go-go dancers be-bopping on top of their speakers for a big crowd.

My favorite part was probably the ceiling light show ~ the "Fremont Street Experience" ~ the last time I saw it, the show was really lame. This time they used excellent music and the images were uber-cool, very retro, and so psychedelic. Whales turned into paisley swirls of red and blue and then turned back again. Veddy cool!!!

Kathleen Madigan is my new best friend!!! Amy & I saw her show at Harrah's on Thursday night, and she was hilarious. (The best joke was about Celine Dion!) I waited in line afterward to ask her to sign a t-shirt for Wesley ~ she was so nice, *real*, & chatty. This night was probably the best part of the whole trip!

Las Vegas

At the Hoover Dam, Amy shows Woodrow where support lines stretch all the way across the Colorado River, downstream from the dam itself. The day was hot & "breezy" ~ Las Vegas-speak for "gale-force winds; hold onto small children and animals or they'll blow away."

Woodrow's favorite parts were our bad "dam" puns, like, "Let's take the dam tour," "All this dam walking is exhausting," and "Where's the dam souvenir shop? I want a dam postcard!"

Bay Loftis of Philadelphia, Tennessee, journaled on a blog, an online journaling site, while visiting Las Vegas. Bay printed the blog when she returned home and transferred her thoughts onto this page.

supplies: Light, medium, dark gray papers • Teal, gray textured papers (Club Scrap) • Rubber stamps (Club Scrap) • Gray stamping ink (Stewart Superior) • Transparency (3M) • Blue, blue-green pigment pens (Ranger) • Buttons (Junkitz) • Beads • Ribbon • Acrylic star charm

Blog Bulletins

Travelers who enjoy writing in experimental formats might enjoy a blog, short for "Web log," while on the road. A blog is an online journal that can be accessed from any computer with an Internet connection, anywhere in the world. It is a new online trend for modern diarists. You can post instant commentary, upload digital pictures and share your adventures with others.

A blog is easy to create and post to. Try a site like blogger.com that hosts blogs for no charge. Depending on how you set the preferences, your posts can have public access or remain private. Bay Loftis of Philadelphia, Tennessee, tried blogging during a trip to Las Vegas. She went to blogger.com and within five minutes created a blog. Then while traveling, she updated the blog on a daily basis with a trip report. When she returned home, Bay says it was a breeze to cut and paste her blog journaling to create a travel layout. This experiment left Bay hooked on blogging, and she describes the practice as "an easy-to-use, infectious activity with a great sense of community."

free **blog**
web sites

• livejournal.com

• opendiary.com

• xanga.com

• blog-city.com

• blogster.com

• diaryland.com

Notebook Log

A small notebook with a pocket is a great tool for data heads who like to log road-trip details and keep receipts. You can tuck receipts into the pocket as you travel and log basic information such as miles driven and money spent on gas. Leah Blanco Williams of Rochester, New York, kept track of miles driven per state and state gas prices during her move from Missouri to New York. Once ready to create a page about the trip, Leah used graph and chart software to convert the miles driven per state and the cost of gas per state. She then printed the charts and graphs to use as page journaling.

Mileage and gas price statistics jotted into a travel notebook are converted into charts and graphs for journaling on this page by Leah Blanco Williams of Rochester, New York. Leah saved receipts in the notebook sleeve to aid her in making her graphs after her road trip.

supplies: Patterned papers (Paper Loft, Karen Foster, 7 Gypsies) • Metal foil (Magic Scraps) • White mulberry paper • Blue vellum • Alphabet stamps (Leave Memories) • Postcard sticker (Paper Love) • Acrylic paint (Plaid) • Graph Chart software (Microsoft) • Cargo Two SF, Year Supply of Fairy Cakes fonts (scrapvillage.com)

Postcard Impressions

Postcard journaling is a perfect fit for travelers who want to document their memories but are not prolific writers. Buy postcards that catch your eye at stops along the journey, and then fill them out when you have snippets of downtime. Jot down your impressions in a quick, unstructured style to capture the spontaneity of the moment. As you write them, further preserve the time and place by sending the postcards to yourself. You will enjoy recalling trip details by reading the postcards once you return home, plus local stamps and postmarks will augment the messages. In the end, you have a fun combination of journaling and memorabilia to incorporate into your scrapbook pages.

When designing scrapbook layouts with the postcards, showcase both the picture on the front and the writing on the back. Incorporate two-sided viewing of the postcards with interactive ideas. Hinge the cards so they can lift up to reveal journaling, place them in clear plastic or vellum pockets for easy removal, or create a mini postcard book that is tucked into a niche or pocket. Heidi Schueller (Masters '03) displayed postcards she sent to herself while in the Czech Republic by creating an accordion book shown left. She made a plastic sleeve for each postcard and then attached them together with eyelets and twine. The postcard book fits perfectly into a mica pocket on the page (shown below).

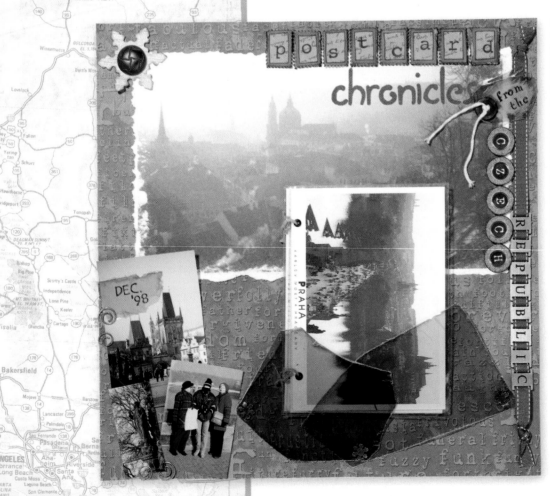

Heidi Schueller (Masters '03) made an accordion book from postcards she sent to herself. The postcards tucked into a mica pocket show and tell of her adventures in the Czech Republic.

supplies: Patterned paper (Deluxe Designs) • Lettering template (Wordsworth) • Stazon black solvent ink (Tsukineko) • Eyelets • Mica (USArtquest) • Snowflake brads (Jo-Ann) • Paper clay (Creative Paperclay) • Button • Fibers • Alphabet stamps (Hero Arts, PSX) • Acrylic paint (Plaid) • Ribbon • Metal letter ribbon charms (Die Cuts With a View) • Tag-Along alphabet (Deluxe Designs) • Cork • Typewriter key letter stickers (EK Success)

Amanda Goodwin of Munroe Falls, Ohio, included a daily rundown of her New York getaway on this page along with memorable moments and sayings.

supplies: Patterned paper (Far and Away) • Transparency • Brads (Creative Imaginations) • Destroy, Book Antiqua and Carpenter ICG fonts (downloaded from the Internet)

travel journaling **inspirations**

Use these prompts to ignite your imagination as you journal on the road.

- Record the basics: who, what, where, when and how.

- Employ all of the five senses to add dimension to the tale.

- Sketch motifs, textures and shapes that catch your eye.

- Draw layout designs and notate color combinations ideas for future use.

- Note memorable historical facts.

- Jot down quotes, snippets and comments from travel companions and tour guides.

- Compare and contrast your hometown with your vacation spot.

- Compose quick character studies of people you have met along the way.

- Write down the humor and the "Murphy's Law" moments that infuse the trip.

- Fill in the blanks for questions such as: "If I only remember one thing from this sight, it would be _____" or "My favorite thing about this day was _____."

- Memorialize the "perfect moments" that you experience.

DESTINATION:

Wild Horses of
Shackleford Banks

North Carolina

Emerald Isle
North Carolina

Fort Macon
Atlantic Beach, NC
Where History Meets Nature

Tucker

emerald isle

north carolina

our vacation

Souvenir-Packed Pages

10 cool ways to include memorabilia on your pages.

by Julie Labuszewski

Boarding passes, ticket stubs, travel brochures, matchbooks, coins and receipts, you collect them all on your travel adventures and then stuff them in your suitcase hoping they will find a place in your vacation album. After all, you're a scrapbooker. You know that a piece of memorabilia can capture a moment in time, document a place you visited or trigger a priceless vacation memory. But how do you incorporate memorabilia onto your layouts? Read on to learn how these scrapbookers discovered breakthrough ways to display and design with mementos.

Destination Brochures

Denise Tucker (Masters '04) was inspired to create this suitcase pocket to hold travel brochures after seeing one designed by Pam Sivage of Georgetown, Texas. For further design inspiration, Denise viewed vintage suitcases online, taking note of leather straps, metal corners and luggage tags. She began by cutting a suitcase shape from foam core to which she adhered crumpled and inked brown paper with decoupage medium. To authenticate the luggage, she hand stitched two strips of faux leather paper and strung them through buckles to create straps. A hand-cut luggage tag is topped with an eyelet and then connected to the strap with twine. Metallic papers adhered with brads become the corners of the luggage. To create a pocket, she cut an opening on the top of the suitcase into which she tucked the brochures. Luggage stickers cut from patterned paper give the suitcase a travel history.

supplies: Foam core • Rustic Ivory paper (Rusty Pickle) • Stamp patterned papers (Rusty Pickle) • Map patterned papers (Design Originals, Me & My Big Ideas) • Faux leather paper (Freckle Press) • Transparency (3M) • Rub-on letters (Making Memories) • Decoupage medium (Plaid) • Paint pens (Krylon) • Brads • Distress Ink (Ranger) • Computer font • Thread

Passports, Stamps & Coins

To document all the countries she and her family have traveled to, Colleen Macdonald of Winthrop, Australia, photocopied pages from her passport, featuring official immigration stamps. She included them on the page along with the retired passport and foreign money, which she displayed in transparent coin holders. She inked the edges of the passport and journaling blocks to match the distressed feel to the page. Rub-on letters identify the location of each photo.

supplies: Patterned paper (Daisy D's) • Rubber stamps (Stampabilities, Inkadinkado, Stamp Deco, Hero Arts) • Nailheads (Beads & Plenty More) • Rub-on letters, watch faces (Li'l Davis) • Coin holders (3L) • Mini brads (Lasting Impressions) • Brown stamping ink (Ranger) • Letter stickers (Sticker Studio, Daisy D's, Li'l Davis)

Beach Finds

"I raided my kids' beach treasure collection bucket for this page," says Jeniece Higgins (Masters '05). On this summer vacation page, she corrals these treasures in clear pockets and label holders. To create the clear pockets, she taped three sides of a page protector together, filled it with sand and shells, then taped the top closed. She mounted the pockets inside label holders that she painted green to match the background paper. Rickrack, ribbon and cheesecloth accent the layout.

supplies: Patterned paper (Rusty Pickle) • Label holder (Li'l Davis) • Acrylic paint (Plaid) • Ribbon (Rusty Pickle) • Rub-on letters (Rusty Pickle, Doodlebug) • Rickrack • Shells • Sand • Driftwood • Cheesecloth • Brads

Tour Memorabilia

Lori Ann Lewis of Des Moines, Iowa, found inspiration for this page from the gift-shop wall she saw on an NBC Studio tour. Colorful blocks and teardrop accents that mimic the NBC logo embellish a pocket that holds an admission ticket, map and brochures. The logo-inspired bright colors are used throughout the page and pop against the black background.

supplies: Black paper (Bazzill) • Purple, red, orange, yellow, green, blue papers • Letter tiles (Creative Imaginations) • Tag (Making Memories) • Tear drop metal embellishment (Scrapyard 329)

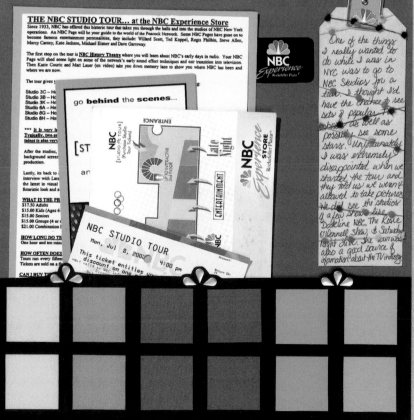

Day One

Journaling on Aug. 3, 2003

Well the trip started out badly (hopefully not a sign as to what is to come). The flight was uneventful and we arrived at the Ft. Lauderdale airport early. We checked in at the Royal Caribbean counter and then got our luggage. We proceeded to wait. Then wait some more. We finally boarded a bus one and a half hours after disembarking from the plane. We then waited another 13 minutes before the bus left the airport.

We finally got on the ship about 3:15. We went to our room and dropped off our bags. We decided to tour the boat. We came back to the room and made some phone calls. At 4:30, we had the Mustering Drill. We decided to go down early. We had to put on our life jackets as we went outside. Since we were one of the first to arrive we were stuck next to the wall with everyone in front of us. It was so hot and in very close quarters. The announcements were made and then repeated in several other languages. We went back to the room and called Grandma and Grandpa while we waited for the ship to leave the port.

At a little after 5:00, we were under way. The way out to the ocean followed a main highway and many of the cars were honking and waving as we pulled away. WOW, we were so excited to be on our first cruise.

Cruise Ship Itinerary

Amy Alvis of Indianapolis, Indiana, found color inspiration for this page from a cruise ship itinerary. The summer colors of light blue and bright yellow set the mood for a nautical page. A pocket with photos of her and her husband holds their boarding passes. A paper strip attached with brads holds the itinerary, allowing it to serve as journaling as well. Rub-on letters on a transparency attached to the bottom of the paper strip sums up her trip—"Paradise Found."

supplies: Blue paper (Bazzill) • Striped patterned paper (KI Memories) • Letter stickers (Doodlebug) • Transparency • Rub-on letters (Making Memories) • Typo font (twopeasinabucket.com)

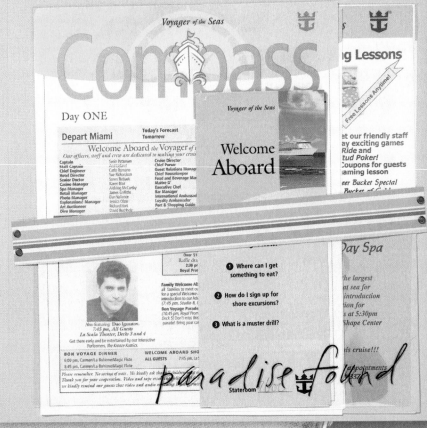

Coins & Tickets

Nic Howard (Masters '05) created a coin holder to display coins, plane tickets, tokens, vouchers and receipts from a day trip to Middle Earth—Wellington, New Zealand. To make the coin holder, Nic used a 1" circle punch to punch holes in 1½" wide strips of cardstock. She then lined up the four strips closely to one another and painted them. After the paint dried, Nic tucked and adhered her memorabilia inside the nooks of the coin holder.

supplies: Brown, light blue papers (Bazzill) • Printed vellum (K & Co.) • Distress Ink (Ranger) • Acrylic paint • Circle punch • Coins • Plane tickets • Token • Receipts • Papyrus, Rockwell fonts (downloaded from the Internet)

Maps & Receipts

Directions scribbled on hotel stationery, gas receipts, interstate maps, a parking permit, receipts and a key card could easily be found on the floor of the car after a long road trip. Cherie Ward of Colorado Springs, Colorado, used all these items to document a road trip with her family. To create the background, she stitched pieces of patterned paper to cardstock and then included the scanned and printed memorabilia. Black and white ribbon that resembles a road is a finishing touch along with an interstate-sign-shaped magnifying glass from a fast-food kid's meal.

supplies: Light green paper • Patterned paper (KI Memories, Creative Imaginations, Rusty Pickle, Mustard Moon, 7 Gypsies) • Rubber stamps (Hero Arts) • Ribbon (Making Memories) • Face Lift font (dafont.com) • Parking permit • Key card • Magnifying glass • Play money • Receipts • Maps

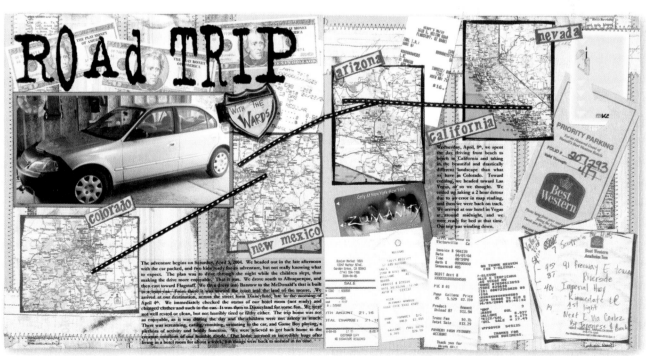

Shopping Brochures

To capture the thrill of shopping in the Grand Cayman, Melissa Smith of North Richland Hills, Texas, created a beach tote to hold shopping brochures. She scanned, reduced and then printed the brochures, which she tucked behind the tote. Beaded trim embellishes the tote while braided raffia forms the handles (see steps below).

supplies: Patterned paper (Rusty Pickle) • Stazon black solvent ink (Tsukineko) • Raffia • Burlap • Seashells • Silk leaves • Beaded fringe • Computer font

Shopping in Paradise

The view coming ashore for shopping at Grand Cayman from the cruise ship was beautiful ... and filled with anticipation of the trinkets to see! When we booked the cruise, we were so focused on the excitement of being on the Disney Magic that we didn't even think about the shopping at our various destinations. Daddy surprised me with this beautiful ring from one of the shops, and one for Sara and Emily, too. The ring is so special, not only because it's beautiful, but it reminds me how generous and loving your daddy is to all of us girls. By the time it came around to getting pictures of the rings to scrap, Sara and Emily, your rings are no where to be found ... is that a ploy to get Dad to take another cruise and replace them? You sneaky girls ... I hope it works!

---

step by step

creating a beach tote pocket

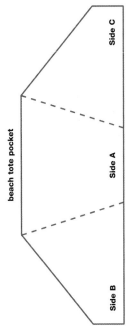

beach tote pocket — Side C, Side A, Side B

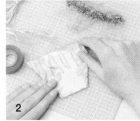
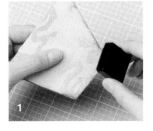

1. Copy pattern shown left (enlarge 300%) and trace onto patterned paper. Cut tote from paper and fold side C and B behind side A. Ink the edges. **2.** Place a double-sided adhesive strip at the top of tote and then adhere raffia strips. **3.** Braid three strips of raffia to form the handle. **4.** Place a double-sided adhesive strip to the back of the tote and then adhere the handle. Embellish front of tote with beaded fringe.

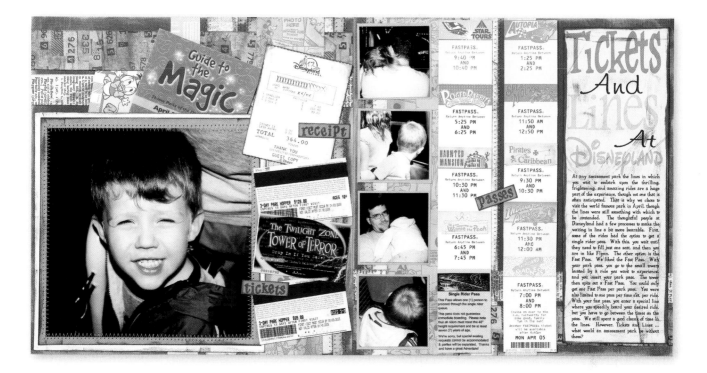

Ride Tickets

When Cherie Ward of Colorado Springs, Colorado, went to Disneyland with her family, she collected ride tickets called FastPasses. "Since they are different colors with different graphics, we thought they would make a great page." Cherie stitched paper together to form a background to which she adhered two rows of FastPasses. To hold brochures and a stroller tag, Cherie made a large pocket that also frames the focal photo. To make the pocket, she stitched the photo onto a larger piece of cardstock then adhered it to the background.

supplies: Purple paper (Bazzill) • Patterned papers (Mustard Moon, Rusty Pickle, 7 Gypsies, Sandylion) • Rubber stamps (Hero Arts) • Walt Disney Script font (dafonts.com) • Conti Street font (mouserfonts.com)

Matchbooks

"I have always collected matchbooks from my travels near and far," says Jeniece Higgins (Masters '05). On this page, she showcases six matchbooks from her trip to Las Vegas with each one opening up to reveal Jeniece's personal account of the day. To create fold-out journaling, Jeniece removed the matches and then cut paper the same width as the matchbook. She used the matchbook fold as a guide for the four folds of the inserts. Playing cards reinforce the casino theme, and the number "2" also is significant. "I liked the number 2 because it was the two of us," says Jeniece.

supplies: Black paper (Provo Craft) • Patterned paper (Making Memories) • Vellum (The Paper Co.) • Threads letters (Me & My Big Ideas) • Label holders (Making Memories) • Ribbon • Playing cards • Matchbooks • Computer font

travel scrapbooks |

get that Shot

10 take-along tips to ensure you'll capture postcard-worthy photos.

by Mike McCarty

Photos are the souvenirs, the sweet reminders of our travels. But while traveling, you may only get one chance at capturing a moment, a landmark or a beautiful sunset—then it is lost forever or until you pass that way again.

Whether you are using a digital format or conventional film, use these techniques to capture extraordinary snapshots that will tell of your travel adventures and take you back there again and again.

use people and objects to establish scale

When the subject of your photo is mammoth or miniscule in size, you can communicate that in your photos by including another object as a comparison. The other object should be common and of recognizable size. People and cars are examples that work well in contrast to larger subjects. For smaller items, coins or currency can be used. Arrange the elements in close proximity to each other.

The small scale of this house is immediately established with a small boy crowded on the front steps.

The immensity of this landmark can be fully appreciated when the viewer notices the people near the base.

PHOTO: MARK LEWIS

PHOTO: HEIDI DILLON

Move in close and allow the contrasting light to emphasize the textures of the subject as seen on this photo shown right.

Identify a theme you want to highlight and focus on that alone. The sharp focus makes the detailing apparent. By centering on the theme, the symmetry of this architecture is underscored.

PHOTO: CHERIE WARD

PHOTO: HEIDI DILLON

fill the frame with your subject

When you want to showcase a single subject, emphasize it by eliminating all other objects from the image. Frame the subject using pleasing lines or shapes you find in the subject itself. Hold the camera up to your eye and look around through the viewfinder before you make an exposure. Where you can, walk around the object to find its best aspect. Pay extra attention to how light and shadows fall on your subject while trying to eliminate any background that might be distracting.

zoom in to capture details

At the longer setting, the zoom acts as a telephoto to magnify a portion of the image you would normally see. Use this when it is just not possible to get closer to your subject and where you want to eliminate other surrounding distractions. Take care at closer telephoto ranges as motion from you or the subject will also be magnified and can blur the image.

At a shorter range, your zoom may act as a slightly wide-angle lens. This is an excellent way to capture groups, landscapes or objects in close quarters. Objects close to the lens will be emphasized over those in the background. Use this effect when you have a subject you want to emphasize and where there are also surrounding portions of the scene you want to include.

Use your zoom in the telephoto range to magnify a portion of the image and focus on a distant subject. This technique is great for capturing the details of subjects such as wildlife that you may not otherwise be able to get close to.

PHOTO: DONETTE BUXTON

utilize magic light

The natural light around dawn and dusk creates warmth and a magical glow in an otherwise average photo. The low-level sun will bring rich colors and elongated shadows. In such conditions you must work quickly because the quality and quantity of light can change dramatically in less than a minute. Given that early and late-day light are dim, you may want to use a tripod or other support to minimize camera movement at slower shutter speeds.

Sometimes the subject of the photo is in fact the sunrise or sunset itself. These can be tricky as your camera may not read the light as you might expect. For the best exposure, take several shots.

You might try a mix of flash with this natural "magic light." This technique can help you emphasize your subject. The flash will add a bit of sparkle to the eyes of your subject, help to fill in harsh shadows and it will also "freeze" the movement of your subject.

PHOTO: TOM PRUDENCE

Look for subjects that are enhanced by the golden quality of early and late-day light. Be prepared to take the photo when the light looks pleasing, but don't wait for it to get better or you may miss it. Long shadows from a sun low in the sky add interest.

Shooting with the intense setting sun behind you can fool your camera's meter into underexposure. To avoid this, aim your camera at an area in the sky away from the direct sun, lock that exposure, recompose, and then snap the photo. Take numerous shots while the light changes and choose the best one later.

PHOTO: CELY LEWIS

add interest with a creative composition

A common subject can be made interesting by shooting it from an unusual vantage point. Look for different, higher or lower positions from which to take your shot. Look for compositions using foreground or background that give insight into your main subject. Often, even slight movement to the left, right, up or down will bring elements into the photo as well as exclude elements that don't contribute to the best visual.

PHOTO: PAMELA JAMES

PHOTO: HEIDI DILLON

Seek out interesting foreground or background objects that complement the story you want to tell such as these distant canyons seen through a rustic fence. Strong lines and good arrangement in the viewfinder make for an interesting photo.

Watch for an opportunity to capture your subject from a non-traditional viewpoint. Choose an angle that will tell a story that is not often told such as this peek at a city through a clock.

rule of thirds

The rule of thirds, an invention of Renaissance painters, is a guideline you can use to compose a masterpiece photo. Imagine your viewfinder is divided horizontally with two equidistant lines and then also vertically in the same manner. Place your main subject at an intersection of two lines. If there is a strong visual line in your scene, use the lines themselves. Experiment by moving your camera around a bit before you shoot, or take several shots to find the best composition.

PHOTO: JODI AMIDEI

Imagine this scene is divided into three sections vertically and horizontally. These lines and their intersections will provide guides to compose your photo.

use a vertical or horizontal angle

When the major focus of your scene has far more vertical than horizontal orientation or vice versa, emphasize it. Try rotating the camera 90 degrees to frame it in a vertical shot. It may feel a bit awkward, especially if you are not accustomed to holding your camera in this manner. Can't choose between horizontal or vertical? Maybe creatively cropping the final print in a square or other shape is the answer.

PHOTO: MYRON LOWE

PHOTO: MYRON LOWE

Eliminate surrounding portions of the scene by going vertical with your lens as in this Eiffel Tower photo. This orientation will emphasize the height of your subject.

Choose the format that will emphasize some aspect of your photo such as the horizontal and converging lines of the wall, river and boats in this photo.

try an extreme angle

You might find that just a slight change in how you point your lens can make a dramatic difference in the result. Get closer to the main subject and allow it to span the entire image or tilt your lens upward or downward. Don't worry about keeping the horizon level. Allow lines in the shapes of your subject to draw the viewer's eye into and through the photo.

PHOTO: HEIDI DILLON

Shoot your subject from an oblique angle as in this photo of the Eiffel Tower. Orient your image slightly off-axis to the horizon for even further impact.

Position yourself closer to the subject and point the lens upward to emphasize height. Branches in the photo serve to draw viewers to the clock.

PHOTO: BARB HOGAN

PHOTO: MYRON LOWE

Shoot from an angle to add the perception of distance such as the perfect lineup of these scooters.

The walls in the photo below converge to one point, conveying the depth and narrowness of the walkway.

PHOTO: JESSIE BALDWIN (MASTERS '05)

capture perspective

A photo is a 2-dimensional representation of our 3-dimensional world. You can use converging and diverging lines in the scene to give your picture perspective and the perception of depth. By composing your photo using a vanishing point (see term below), such as a winding road or river bend, you guide the viewer's eye through the photo.

vanishing point

Vanishing point is the effect we experience when parallel lines appear to meet in the distance. This conveys the perception of depth as in these cemetery and river photos. The grave markers appear to converge in the distance. And while we know this does not occur, it seems to carry our eyes well beyond what we can see. Though we cannot see where the river continues to flow, the river bend visually carries our eye around the corner.

PHOTO: MYRON LOWE

PHOTO: MYRON LOWE

Position the lines evident in your scene so as to draw your viewer in and through the image. Frame the image into thirds (see p. 44).

Use perpendicular lines in the scene to convey depth as the crosses in this photo. The lines drawn by repetitive objects add the perception of width. Use other elements of good composition such as the rule of thirds (p. 44) and vanishing point to enhance the final image.

PHOTO: TOM PRUDENCE

Be prepared to record human activity by having your camera around your neck and ready to go. The adventure of this person crawling across a log to cross the river makes for a more interesting photo than just the river itself.

PHOTO: THOM JAMES

Include yourself in the photo by using your camera's self-timer. Position your subjects closer to the camera and use the landscape or a landmark as an interesting backdrop.

PHOTO: JESSIE BALDWIN (MASTERS '05)

Seek out a shot to convey the emotion of that moment. People are often able to recall more about situations where some human aspect was included in the photo.

get people in the picture

The common "we were here" picture is a simple and memorable record of one or more people posing with a landmark. Pose your subjects close to the landmark to emphasize size. You can also use the landmark as a background with your subjects positioned closer to the camera. Position your subjects to one side rather than in the middle, and focus your lens on them. Recording people in an activity will add emotional appeal.

PHOTO: JOANNA BOLICK (MASTERS '04)

Imagine a line running through the scene that you can follow, and take a series of photos that can later be spliced together.

capture a vast scene with a panorama

Nothing captures an expansive scene as well as a panorama, but sometimes your entire shot just won't fit into the standard rectangular format. In the simplest form, you can perform an extreme crop on a normal print. Find a straight visual through the scene and crop extraneous top and bottom portions of the print.

   Getting slightly more complex—you can splice together a set of photos to form one elongated photo. Identify a line you want to follow through the scene and take numerous shots, overlapping each slightly with the previous shot. Maybe a complete 360-degree panorama tells the best story. Use a non wide-angle setting and keep the camera level for the greatest results. This is best done with the aid of a tripod. If you don't have a tripod, improvise by propping your camera on another object.

PHOTO: HEIDI DILLON

Special equipment is not needed for a panorama. You can take a photo with the idea that you will later horizontally crop out portions of the scene that don't contribute to the message you want to convey.

quick flip books and page pockets

Flip books and memento pockets are fast and easy ways to turn stacks of photos and memorabilia into awesome scrapbook pages. Flip Flop Fasteners from Destination Stickers and Stamps make creating flip elements that incorporate extra photos and journaling a breeze.

Karen Foster's Sticky Pockets, also seen in the layout, make including mementos on your page safe and easy. Simply peel off the backing and apply. The pockets are clear so contents show through. Pockets come in several styles, with three different sizes per pack.

Use Flip Flop Fasteners from Destination Stickers and Stamps to make photos and journaling flip open, up or down or to create a flip book such as Jenn Brookover (Masters '05) did on this page.

supplies: Patterned paper (Making Memories, Scrapworks) • Flip Flop Fasteners (Destination) • Sticky Pocket (Karen Foster) • Metal flower (Making Memories) • Letter stickers (American Crafts) • Brads • Ribbon • Rust font (Chatterbox)

step by step

flip-flop flip book

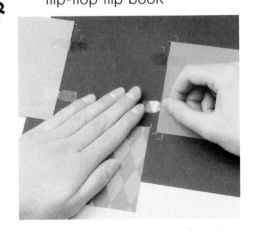

Flip Flop Fasteners act like hinges—attach the bottom half of the clear poly strip to your page background and the top to a flip element as shown in the inset above.

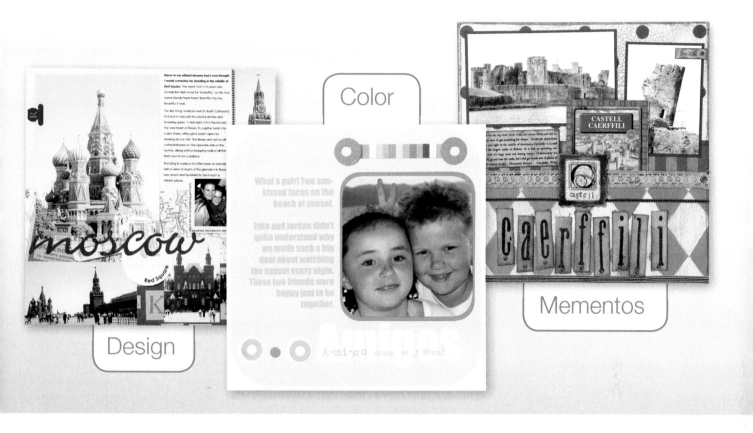

Color

Design

Mementos

common threads

Orchestrate quick, flawless travel
albums with common design, color
or mementos.   by Michelle Pesce (Masters '04)

You're home now. The blissful days of vacation sit in front of you in the form
of stacks and stacks of photos. Despite the smile that lights up your face as you
flip through the images, the thought of coming up with original designs for each
page of your travel scrapbook quickly can eliminate your after-vacation bliss.

A travel album doesn't have to be intimidating if you use one of the common-threads principles outlined in this article. These three principles teach you
that you don't need to redesign every layout to make it outstanding. In fact,
these principles make a project not only go faster, but also give an album a more
cohesive feel.

The principles are simple, just pick one: Use a similar design structure for
each page; establish a consistent color scheme; or pepper the pages with common mementos you picked up along the trip. Do this and your album will be
ready quickly so you can start daydreaming about your next trip and your next
travel album. Read on to learn how three dynamic travel albums were created
using these common-threads principles.

common thread:
Design

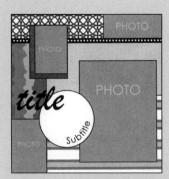

A consistent design provides a structural blueprint to make page assembly quick and easy. A common design thread can create cohesion when the following cannot: sets of photos without a discernible color scheme or photos and memorabilia that hail from several different locales, each with their own temperament. Use your design to set the mood—busy and whirlwind or graphic and serene.

Moscow
Sheila Doherty (Masters '05)

In this album, Sheila uses a fairly structured design but adds variety via different patterned and colored papers. She chose a flexible design that she modified to complement each page's specific photos. "I wanted something that would give me the flexibility to incorporate several different patterns of paper on one page," she says. The similar design keeps the page construction easy while the design flexibility keeps the album interesting.

supplies: Patterned papers (7 Gypsies, American Traditional, Chatterbox, Déjà Views by C-Thru Ruler, Design Originals, Li'l Davis, Paper Love, Rusty Pickle) • Tan paper • Index tabs (Autumn Leaves) • Foam stamps, photo anchors, brads (Making Memories) • Alphabet stamps (PSX) • Circle punch (Marvy) • Versamark watermark stamping ink (Tsukineko) • Acrylic paint (Plaid) • Ribbon (Li'l Davis, Making Memories, Michaels) • Embossing powder (Embossing Arts) • Ticket stub • Negative strip • Bickley Script font (linotype.com) • Century Gothic font (fonts.com)

How it works:

create unified titles and journaling blocks
For each title treatment, Sheila used the same handcut font in the same size and coupled it with uniform circles cut from the same paper, stamped with the same image and printed with the date. A photo (always of people) bordered by captions is present on every page. While the papers and colors vary, the width of the caption strips and the font size and type are consistent. Her journaling blocks also incorporate a consistent font color and style choice.

size and place photos consistently
Even though each page is unique in terms of photo location, the size and placement of Sheila's photos are carefully orchestrated. Each focal photo is standard in size—8 x 5" or 8 x 6"—and positioned to enhance the orientation. Two smaller photos are added in opposite corners on the diagonal (upper right and lower left), and placed flush with the edges of the page. Through size and the careful choice of background papers, the focal photo of each page is clearly defined.

At first glance, the similar design structure inherent to these pages is subtle. Study the pages further to detect consistent title and journaling treatments, similar photo sizing and placement, common embellishments and a successful mix of patterned papers. All these attributes made creating this album easier, unified the layouts for a cohesive feel and resulted in an album that is impossible not to enjoy.

pick common embellishments

The placement of the embellishments may differ, but Sheila incorporates a few of the same accents on each page to establish continuity throughout the album. First, a negative-strip tag on each page is stamped with letters and tied with a coordinating ribbon. A length of narrow black checked ribbon defines an edge where two different papers meet. Photo turns draw attention to the captioned photo mats, and index tabs on each focal photo reference the page theme.

mix patterned papers successfully

Sheila's expert use of patterned papers in a style similar to color-blocking contributes a more subtle design similarity between her pages. She balances the more complex patterns with blocks of simpler or plain papers, offering the eye a chance to rest and her photos a chance to stand out against a simpler background. Her choice of patterned papers reflects the travel and old-world themes of her album while highlighting the colors in her photos.

common thread:
Color

Using common colors and patterns is one of the simplest ways to unify an album. This technique allows for flexibility when choosing decorative elements yet still maintains cohesion. It will cut down your design time by automating your paper choices. Look at common color themes in your photos (clothing, sunsets, water) and color wheel combinations to help determine a working palette.

Puerta Vallarta

Jodi Heinen (Masters '05)

Jodi made this album a snap by choosing one patterned paper and two solid complements. "I laid all my pictures out and chose two colors that seemed to be a common thread in nearly all my pictures—blue and orange," she says. These choices beautifully complement skin tones, sunset skies, blue jeans and ocean waters. Then, for each page, she created a three-tone monochromatic color scheme. In addition to her color choices, Jodi employs strong design elements such as simple lines, shape (curves and circles) and consistent title and text treatments to further enhance the album's continuity.

supplies: Patterned papers (KI Memories) • Rust, navy papers (Prism) • Corner rounder, circle punch (Marvy) • Impact, Times New Roman fonts (fonts.com) • Harting font (dafont.com)

How it works:

set the mood with color

Color, more than any other design element, has the ability to evoke emotion, and Jodi's soft pastels reflect the carefree relaxation of a tropical vacation. Orange communicates warmth, the playfulness of youth and, in stronger shades, energy and excitement. Blue is symbolic of calm, serenity and peacefulness. What colors stand out in your photos and what emotions do they conjure up about your journey?

minimize the number of patterns/solids

One lively patterned paper that reflects the many different colors contained in the photos forms the cornerstone of Jodi's color scheme. This serves as another inspiration for her solid color choices, of which she chose only two. To ensure a perfect match to the patterned paper, Jodi used computer-generated colors for the page backgrounds. She printed out a sample palette to guarantee that her backgrounds would coordinate perfectly with the colors in the patterned paper.

What a pair! Two sun-kissed faces on the beach at sunset.

Jake and Jordan didn't quite understand why we made such a big deal about watching the sunset every night. These two friends were happy just to be together.

Amigos

A•mi•go *noun. m., f.* friend

Chica

Chi•ca *adj.* - small, little *f.* girl

Jordan quickly adapted to vacation mode. Here she is in her sun visor, tropical shirt, sea shell necklace and slightly sun-burned cheeks. This little girl is definitely a tourist!

Ciudad

Ci•u•dad *noun.* Center of population, commerce and culture

Puerto Vallarta is a hustling metropolis with a population of 300,000. Somehow this city retains the feel of a traditional Mexican village. The city is surrounded by mountains on one side and the ocean on the other. Puerto Vallarta has something for everyone - beautiful beaches and weather, great shopping and friendly people.

Jodi's effective use of color as a common thread is not the only thing that unifies this album. She also captures the eye with a simple, consistent design. Jodi uses similar title and journaling treatments. Each page is unified via curved features whether they are page or photo corners or circular accents. The softer, rounded lines in the accents contrast nicely against the linear nature of the patterned paper she chose, which not only infuses the layouts with color, but also acts as a simple and clean design element throughout her pages.

carry through color via accents and elements

A patterned paper with so many colors could easily draw the focus of the page away from the photos, but the understated use of the colorful pattern as accent strips and borders ensures that the effect enhances rather than distracts. A few small circle elements reinforce the overall color scheme. The tone-on-tone character of the title treatments and journaling blocks strengthens the impact of the dominant color without marring the simplicity of the overall design.

find a successful color combination

Another factor that contributes to the success of Jodi's album design is the relationship between her main color choices. Orange and blue are complementary colors, and therefore a powerful color combination. Split-complementary and triadic combinations can be equally successful. Consulting a color wheel will help you determine successful combinations from the common colors found in your photos. It also might suggest fresh, new color combinations to try.

common thread:

Mementos

All the fun memorabilia you collect on a trip definitely deserve a place in your album, especially when they serve as a unifying theme. Brochures, ticket stubs, hotel stationery and foreign currency all can become unique design elements. While these things can be fun and quirky additions, it's safe to assume that the majority of them are not made from archival materials, therefore care must be taken to make them safe for use on your pages.

Castle Tour

Trudy Sigurdson (Masters '03)

Trudy collected the visually appealing and information-packed brochures from all the castles she visited and integrated them into her pages for a fresh, unified look. Her brochures are all still accessible should she want to view them in the future. They add the only splash of color in the otherwise monochromatic, antiqued color scheme reflecting of her page subjects. In addition to the brochures and consistent color scheme, Trudy also uses the same black-and-white photo style, similar title treatments and common embellishments on each page.

supplies: Patterned papers (Daisy D's) • Cream, tan, brown papers (Bazzill) • Handmade paper (Scrapbook Sally) • Foam stamps, acrylic paint (Making Memories) • Alphabet stamps (Hampton Arts, My Sentiments Exactly, PSX) • Walnut ink (Fiberscraps) • Stamping ink (Ranger) • Brads (Scrap Arts) • Wooden frames (Prima) • Ribbon • Twill tape • Cotton lace • Codex font (linotype.com) • Florina font (downloaded from the Internet) • JSL Ancient font (dafont.com)

How it works:

choose mementos of uniform size

These brochures are standard in size. This consistency makes them an ideal choice because they were easy to integrate into a uniform page design. Other uniform-sized mementos are business cards, newspaper mastheads and stationery. If you have mementos of different sizes, such as tickets, consider enlarging or reducing them on a color copier and printing them on acid-free paper to make them all a consistent size.

include mementos in the page design

Since mementos vary in appearance, finding a consistent use for them on your pages establishes unity. All of Trudy's brochures are nestled into pockets edged with antiqued lace, with a bit of the brochure showing above the pocket's edge. Pockets or other interactive elements keep mementos such as these accessible. One-sided mementos can be transformed into unique accents, journaling-block backgrounds, tags or parts of other interactive elements.

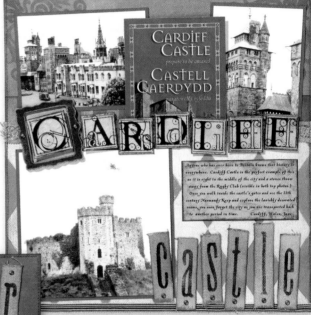

Trudy unified this travel album through her choice of mementos and also through the layout design. She chose a classic color scheme and timeless feel with textures that convey the antiquity and quiet strength in the castles. By unifying these elements, she achieves cohesion despite the fact that each brochure is different in color and style.

address safety concerns

Most paper-based mementos are not archival and can contain acid, which is damaging to photographs, and also lignin, which potentially can damage photographs. Protect your scrapbooks against acid by treating mementos with de-acidification spray to neutralize the acid. Or color-copy mementos onto acid-free, lignin-free paper. At the very least, make sure mementos are not physically touching any of your photographs. You can also seal smaller items into archival clear-plastic pockets that can be affixed directly to your page.

seek location-appropriate memorabilia

When deciding on a common-thread memento, think about the unique characteristics of the place you are visiting. In Trudy's pages, she chose stately brochures full of wonderful details from the castles she visited. Maybe in Germany you would choose beer mats, in China you could pick up chopstick wrappers or in London you might grab matchbooks from famous pubs.

Have Tips, Will Travel

Six pages packed full of scrapbooker-savvy travel knowledge—don't leave home without it.

by Darlene D'Agostino

Have an Itinerary

For some travelers, an itinerary is a major travel "don't" as they prefer to have spontaneous adventures. But, if you can be persuaded to map out a plan, there are several scrapbooking benefits, says Natalie Abbott, co-owner of Creative Impressions. Besides helping her family determine the vacation budget and the amount of film to bring, an itinerary also is an "essential" journaling tool that Natalie refers to upon returning home. "(On an itinerary) everything is organized with locations, correct spellings of places we were and dates," she says.

To help plan an itinerary, buy a travel guide and visit destination Web sites. These also are great resources if you enjoy including travel trivia or details about the places you have visited in your scrapbooks. Some guides to consider are *Insight Guides* (Langenscheidt), *Time Out* (Time Out), *Frommer's* (Wiley), *Eyewitness* (DK), *Fodor's* (Fodor's Travel), *Rough Guide* (Penguin), *Let's Go* (Let's Go), *Footprint Handbooks* (Footprint) and *Lonely Planet* (Lonely Planet).

Find The Local Scrapbook Store

Who has the perfect location-specific travel products? The local scrapbook store (LSS) of your chosen destination. "I always scope the locations of the LSS when I travel and print a map to it (and the phone number in case I get lost)," says Susan Merrel of Starkville, Mississippi. "I also take a hard-sided paper carrier to carry home any finds."

Pack Photo-Friendly Clothing

"I like to preplan pages down to the clothes that people will be wearing in the photos. I feel like shirts with writing detract from the people, so I make sure that everyone in the family has solid-colored shirts before a trip. I usually choose two or three colors (navy, white and khaki, for example) and pack only those colors for the whole family." — Kelli Noto (Masters '03)

Film Speed   Find film speed confusing? Try these film-selection guidelines courtesy of Ken Trujillo, Memory Makers photographer.

slow (100 – 200 ISO) *landscapes, inanimate objects, outdoor events on sunny days* This film requires a lot of light; without it, prints may be dark and blurry. Because it requires more time to absorb light, it is very important to keep the camera still when shooting to prevent blurry photos—use a tripod if possible.

medium (400 ISO) *overcast/shady outdoor images, natural window-light portraits, in conjunction with a long zoom lens* This speed of film is great for general use because you don't have to worry about light as much. If you will be in a variety of situations, this film speed is a good choice.

fast (800 ISO) *fast-moving subjects in low light, when using a zoom lens in low light, in dimly lit situations without a tripod* Faster film requires less light to produce a clear image. It's great for dimly lit situations such as a fireworks display, a beach sunset or candlelit dinner.

Use slow speed film in bright light.

Use fast speed film in low light.

Packing **Film**

Follow these guidelines to keep your film safe.

Keep film in carry-on Never pack unexposed film in checked luggage, says the Transportation Security Administration (TSA), as the radiation will destroy it. According to the TSA, X-ray machines that screen carry-on baggage at the passenger security checkpoint will not affect undeveloped film under 800 ISO.

"If the same roll of film is exposed to X-ray inspections more than five times before it is developed, however, damage may occur," according to the TSA Web site (tsa.gov/public/index). Request a hand-inspection for your film if it has passed through the X-ray four times.

Kelli Noto (Masters '03) puts all of her film into a large plastic zipper bag so it is easy for airport personnel to identify. Natalie Abbott of Creative Impressions recommends removing film from its packaging and placing it in a plastic container to expedite hand-checking. Be aware that international airports may not honor hand-check

requests. The TSA recommends contacting foreign airport security offices to request a manual inspection. While the TSA cautions against lead-lined bags (the bags themselves require inspection), it does advise considering this option if traveling abroad.

Customs concerns The Professional Photographers of America (PPA) says if you are traveling with average equipment and 20 to 30 rolls of film, getting through customs should not be a problem. If you are taking professional equipment, you may have to prove you bought it stateside. A sales receipt should work as proof.

Keep film cool and dry Film is heat-sensitive; store it in a cool, dry place, out of direct sunlight, recommends the PPA. If traveling by car to warmer climates, keep film in the trunk or in a dry cooler, Kelli says. If in a hotel, store unused film in the fridge, says Allison Orthner of Calgary, Alberta, Canada.

Film **Buying**

Use these tips to determine when to buy film and how much to buy.

Buy film before you go Film not only can be expensive on the road (especially if traveling abroad), the selection can be limited, says Natalie Abbott, co-owner of Creative Impressions.

Buy twice the amount you need Film, although perishable, will keep for a long time, says Allison Orthner of Calgary, Alberta, Canada, so it's better to have too much than not enough. Kelli Noto (Masters '03) takes, on average, two rolls for each day. Natalie plans for a minimum of one 36-exposure roll per day.

Ratio method Reader Kate Thaete of Seattle, Washington, uses the following formula to determine her vacation film needs: One roll per day, per three to four people. If you're traveling for five days and traveling with five others, take 10 rolls. Always round up, she says.

Photos You know you're going to have piles of photos. Use these ideas to keep track of your beautiful memories.

label enlargements "If I am cropping and adjusting 100 photos in my photo software, it can be hard to remember just which ones I wanted to enlarge once I upload to an online developer," says Emily Tyner of Charlotte, North Carolina. "Therefore, I save each image with a notation of size (i.e.: Eiffel Tower 8 x 10")."

burn images to cd As you travel, have digital images burned to CD at a local photo finisher, says Lynn Brown of Boyds, Maryland. This frees up memory on your digital camera and also makes sharing photos easy—have multiple CDs burned to give to family or friends.

mark canisters/developing sleeves Label all of your film canisters sequentially, date them and add a small trip detail, says Michelle Birch of Rexburg, Idaho. When you develop the film, mark the corresponding developing sleeves with the same information, and your photos will be pre-organized with details and in chronological order.

Film

Quick tips for keeping track of your film while on the road.

divide exposed and unexposed film Mark clear plastic zipper bags across the top with red and green electrical tape for exposed and unexposed film, respectively, says Linda De Los Reyes of Los Gatos, California. Marking the tops of the bags makes it fast and easy to deposit used film and grab a new roll while on the go.

take mail-in envelopes for photo developing Cut down on space and eliminate the risk of film being ruined by airport X-ray machines by mailing exposed film to a photo finisher from the road, says Lynn Brown of Boyds, Maryland. Once home, happy memories will be waiting to greet you.

Memorabilia

A scrapbooker cannot resist grabbing reminders from a trip. Keep your brochures, matchboxes, napkins and other mementos together and safe with these tips:

keep it organized Trip mementos can stack up quickly, says Kari Hansen-Daffin, craft editor. Take enough zipper bags or envelopes for each day of your trip and a permanent marker. Label each bag or envelope by date and place(s) and add memorabilia as you go, she says. You can even add exposed film to help keep your photos organized. Kari keeps all of this safe inside a Caren's Crafts accordion file.

memento journal Add mementos to your travel journal by securing them with repositionable glue, says Manon Dufour of Chibougamau, Quebec, Canada. As Manon writes about each adventure, she adds any related souvenirs such as ticket stubs, postcards or brochures to the journal. It keeps the mementos safe, organized and it inspires her journaling. Once home, she transfers any items that she wishes to scrapbook to a travel album. If possible, she grabs doubles so she can keep her travel journal complete as well.

don't fret about wear and tear "I actually don't worry about brochures getting damaged," says Samantha Walker (Masters '05). "This might sound funny, but attraction maps, little brochures—those things get used, so I kind of like the creases and wrinkles in them. It shows that they traveled with me."

preserve as you go Carry a de-acidification spray with you to pre- serve paper mementos as you go, advises Julie Johnson (Masters '05). Try Preservation Technologies Archival Mist from EK Success or Make It Acid-Free from Krylon (product is not permitted for air travel because it is a spray can, extremely flammable, and it contains harmful vapors).

scrapbook mementos with these products: Memory Pockets from 3L • Postcard Page and Letter Page from Photopostos • Specialty page protectors from C-Line Products • Sticky Pockets from Karen Foster Design.

Equipment to Take

The following is a checklist to use when packing your equipment for a big trip.

pack the manual Time spent traveling can be time well-spent if you use it to study up on your equipment, says Andrea Steed, owner of Scrap Jazz. "On long car rides you can learn more about your camera and practice some different types of photos along the way," she says.

batteries and cords For manual cameras, buy extra batteries—you may not find what you need while traveling. Fully charge batteries for a digital and take a spare set, says Tricia Morris, president of Club Scrap. Taking the recharger and USB cords is never a bad idea.

specialty lenses Before you pack the specialty lenses, make sure you have your standard lenses: wide-angle (for panoramics, large places such as sports arenas), telephoto (zoom) and macro (detail) lenses.

tripod and a remote Tripods are great for landscape and zoom shots or tough lighting situations, says Samantha Walker (Masters '05). Tripods and a remote also allow you to be a part of a group shot, says Kim Turpin of Victoria, British Columbia, Canada.

back-up camera Take an old camera or buy a few disposable cameras, says Julie Johnson (Masters '05), just in case your camera malfunctions or is stolen.

prepare for a cross-check Before you set foot out the door, empty out your camera bag and check all of your equipment, recommends Jenn Brookover (Masters '05). Be sure to replace or recharge the batteries in your camera and flash.

The Benefits of SLR Cameras

SLR (single lens reflex) cameras require time and patience to learn, but they give a photographer complete control over exposure controls. Other benefits of SLR cameras include:

- interchangeable lenses for creative visual effects
- hard copies of photos in the form of negatives
- less electronic components to worry about, meaning, mechanically, there is less that can go wrong, and there is no chance of accidentally deleting a photo
- only thing to limit enlarging of photos is the film speed used (higher film speed limits enlargement size)

ABOVE INFORMATION FROM KEN TRUJILLO, MEMORY MAKERS PHOTOGRAPHER AND HOW TO TAKE PERFECT SCRAPBOOK PICTURES *(MEMORY MAKERS, 2005) BY JOANN ZOCCHI*

take an extra memory card

These are resounding words of advice from

countless contributors to this issue.

Learn it. Live it. Love it.

The Benefits of Digital Cameras

Digital cameras require no film to capture an image. Instead, images are recorded via pixels and stored in memory. This allows for instant gratification—you know right away if you've gotten a good shot or not, and you can delete the bad ones. Besides this, digital cameras offer the following:
• no need to buy film—less bulk and the ability to switch film-speed settings at the touch of a button
• easier photo-sharing—burn images to a disk or upload to a computer to share with family and friends
• creative control over your photos—enlarge, reduce and crop photos or creatively edit in image-editing software

Ward Off **Thieves**

Adopt these savvy skills from street-smart scrapbookers to keep your camera from getting stolen.

keep your equipment on you "When traveling through Europe alone, I tossed my camera on the chair next to me at a cafe," says Linda De Los Reyes of Los Gatos, California. "A local sat down and started chatting. Later I realized she stole my camera." For air travel, pack your camera in carry-on bags, says Heidi Schueller (Masters '03), who temporarily lost her camera when her luggage didn't arrive in Scotland at the same time that she did.

use disposable cameras at the beach "I have heard of too many people having things stolen on the beach while they played in the water," says Samantha Walker (Masters '05). That's why Samantha uses disposable cameras at the beach. Also, you needn't worry about a stranger stealing it if you ask one to snap a group shot, says Natalie Abbott, co-owner of Creative Impressions. "It's also easier for them to understand if they do not speak your language."

camouflage your goods Camera bags can be thief magnets, says Kelli Noto (Masters '03). Kelli fools would-be filchers by carrying her camera in a soft-sided lunch bag.

Protect your Equipment

label your gear Put a sticker with your contact information on all of your gear, says Colleen Macdonald of Winthrop, Australia. Add your cell phone number, and if a good Samaritan finds it locally, he or she quickly can return it to you, says Susan Merrell of Starksville, Mississippi.

safeguard against lost film Dottie Clark of Belleair, Florida, keeps an index card detailed with her name and address in her camera bag. Each time she loads a new roll of film, she photographs the card. That way, should she lose the film in developing, the photo finisher will have her contact information.

protect from heat and humidity Protect your camera by wrapping it in a clear plastic bag (cut a hole for the lens) secured with a rubber band. Each evening, place exposed rolls of 35mm film on a table in your air-conditioned hotel room, recommends the Professional Photographers of America. It will return the film to a more desirable humidity level before it is resealed in its air-tight container. In the morning, reseal the film in the plastic containers.

buy a voltage converter If traveling abroad, find out if you will need a voltage adaptor for charging batteries, says Kim Turpin of Victoria, British Columbia, Canada. Be sure to get the correct adaptor, otherwise you can damage your equipment.

use wrist and neck bands Always use your camera's protective straps to help prevent yourself from accidentally dropping it.

reader idea gallery

59 new travel page ideas you can use in your scrapbook today!

Globetrotters

Nic Howard (Masters '05)

Nic created a befitting backdrop for this page with pieces of globe patterned paper. She cropped three photos to represent the fact that Thom and Pamela James of Ventura, California, (shown in the photo) are world travelers. She used deckle scissors and photo corners to create a format reminiscent of old-fashioned travel postcards.

supplies: Tan, green, black, white papers (Bazzill) • Patterned paper (Paper Love) • Deckle scissors • Distress ink (Ranger) • Computer fonts • White rickrack • Photo corners

PHOTOS: MYRON LOWE, PAMELA JAMES, COMSTOCK IMAGES, GETTY IMAGES

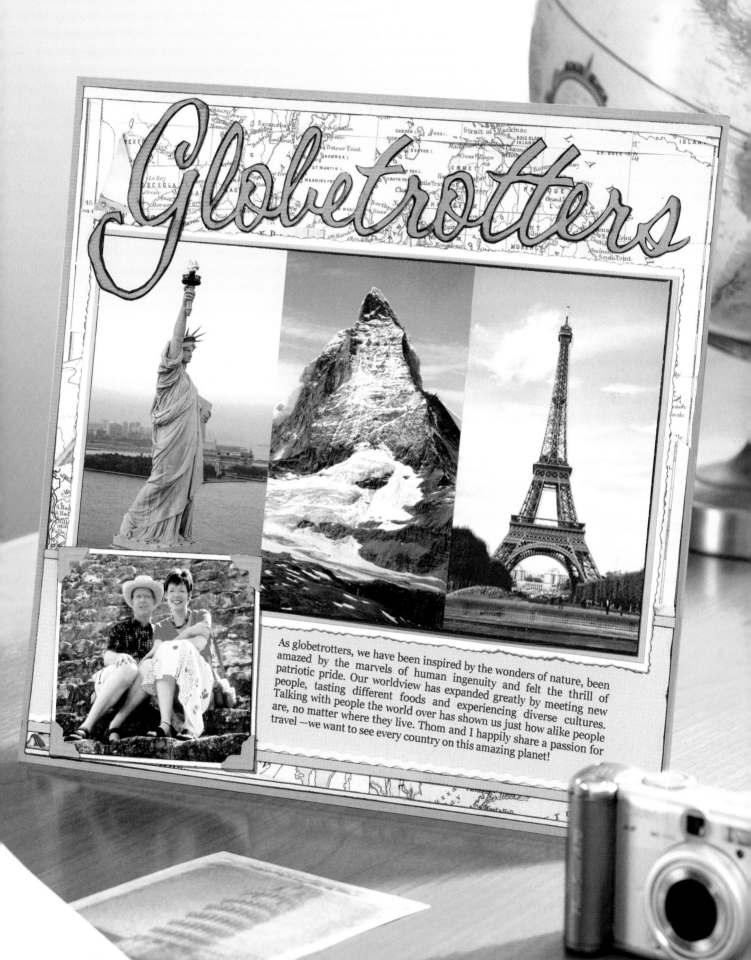

Globetrotters

As globetrotters, we have been inspired by the wonders of nature, been amazed by the marvels of human ingenuity and felt the thrill of patriotic pride. Our worldview has expanded greatly by meeting new people, tasting different foods and experiencing diverse cultures. Talking with people the world over has shown us just how alike people are, no matter where they live. Thom and I happily share a passion for travel —we want to see every country on this amazing planet!

The Lights of Victoria

Sharon Whitehead (Masters '04)

Sharon showcased day and night photos of the historical parliament buildings in Victoria, British Columbia, Canada. Her enlarged panoramic shot is accented with a filmstriplike border of daytime pictures. She created her title using stickers and a computer font cut from paper with a craft knife.

supplies: Navy, sienna, yellow papers (Bazzill) • Ribbon (Making Memories) • Metallic leafing pen (Krylon) • Mini bottle cap letter • Foam adhesive • Computer fonts

I Love New York

Amanda Goodwin, Munroe Falls, Ohio

Throughout her travels, Amanda keeps an eye out for interesting details full of scrapbook potential. Here, she used an embroidered patch as an embellishment and wrote her journaling on an actual postcard she picked up on her trip. Her title was created with acrylic paint and foam stamps. She accented the top of the page with tied ribbons.

supplies: Black, red papers (Bazzill) • Ribbon • Foam stamps • Photo turns • Acrylic paint (Making Memories) • Twill tape • Letter stickers (Chatterbox) • Square punch • Souvenir patch • Postcard • Zig pen (EK Success) • Label maker (Dymo)

Colorful Colorado

Terri Bradford, Henderson, Colorado

Terri documented her great love for Colorado with landscape photos taken during the day and at sunset. For the smaller detail shots, she distressed the edges of the tightly cropped photos with sandpaper. The title block was created by layering an envelope, photos, computer-printed phrases and 3-D letters with foam adhesive.

supplies: Blue, green papers • Page pebble • 3-D letters (K & Co.) • Twine • Envelope (Chatterbox) • Computer fonts

Forty Miles

J.J. Killins, Redondo Beach, California

This layout documents a journey across the streets of New York. J.J.'s list-style journaling details the sightseeing. She cut the title from paper using a craft knife and concealed more journaling behind folded paper anchored with photo turns.

supplies: Yellow, green paper • Patterned papers (Provo Craft, PSX) • Alphabet stamps (PSX) • Ribbon • Stamping ink (Clearsnap) • Tag (Making Memories) • Ring (7 Gypsies) • Brads (Jo-Ann) • Andale Mono font (myfonts.com) • Punchlabel and Jikharev fonts (momscorner4kids.com)

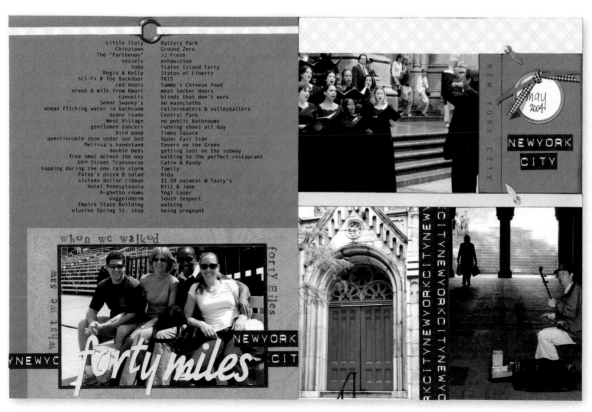

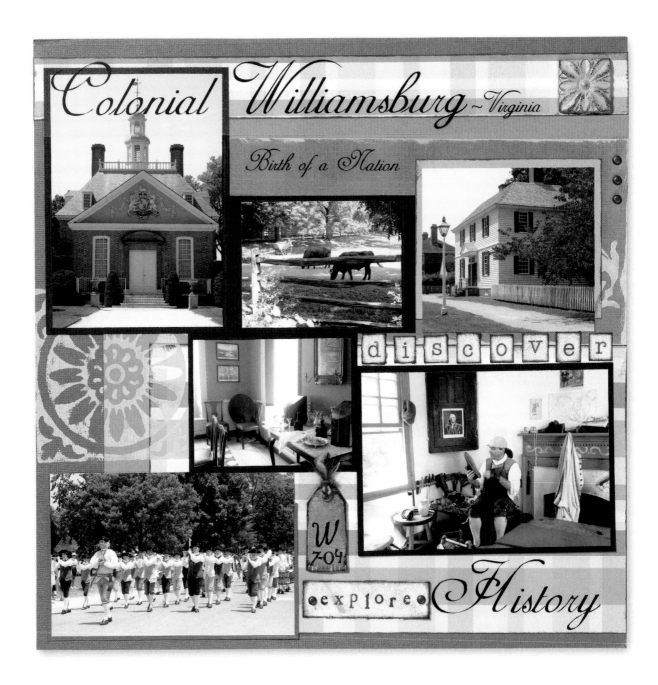

Colonial Williamsburg

Patti Milazzo, Lexington, South Carolina

For the first page of her travel album about Colonial Williamsburg, Virginia, Patti combined several photos. For the background, she inked the edges of patterned paper, painted the edges of solid paper and layered both on brown paper. Using foam stamps and acrylic paint, she then stamped images onto the backgrounds. She printed the title on a transparency and placed it over photos and the background.

supplies: Brown, black, rust, olive papers (Bazzill) • Patterned paper (Chatterbox) • Floral foam stamp (Making Memories) • Brads (Making Memories) • Fabric letters • Rub-ons • Clay • Fiber • Alphabet and number stamps (PSX) • Stamping inks (Clearsnap, Rubber Stampede) • Acrylic paint (Plaid) • Adine Kirnberg font (fontgarden.net)

Sideshow

Lynne Rigazzio-Mau, Channahon, Illinois

Lynne created her design to reflect the artistic flair found in a New Orleans magic shop. Patterned papers and stickers were used to create a border and accents. Her eclectic title is a combination of painted tags, letter stencils, letter stickers and alphabet stamps.

supplies: Black paper • Patterned paper (Rusty Pickle) • Stickers (Embellish It, EK Success) • Alphabet stamps (River City Rubber, Hampton) • Stazon solvent ink (Tsukineko) • Mini dice (Rubber Baby) • Tickets • Key charm (Magic Scraps) • Photo turns • Brads • Acrylic paint (Making Memories)

Niagara Falls

Katy Jurasevich, Crown Point, Indiana

A business trip turned into an opportunity for Katy's first venture across U.S. borders to see the Canadian view of Niagara Falls. She layered patterned papers and vellum across the middle of her page and placed an enlarged photo of the falls on top. She used letter stickers to create the title, placing them directly on her photo. Across the top, she included the date by repeatedly stamping on the dark blue strip of paper.

supplies: Blue papers (Bazzill) • Patterned papers (Chatterbox, 7 Gypsies) • Letter stickers (Making Memories) • Nostalgiques postmark sticker (EK Success) • Lighthouse font (twopeasinabucket.com)

Washington
DC

During the summer of 1997, Scott, Noriko and I went to Washington DC. Dad was there for his summer camp with the Reserves so we stayed with him at the Navy Lodge.

Since this was the first time that Noriko had been to Washington DC (as well as the United States) we tried to see as much of DC as we could. In the evenings we would go to a new restaurant every night. Since Dad went to DC every summer, he knew all the great places to eat.

This was the summer before Kevin and I got married and he didn't have the time to take off of work, so he stayed back in Indiana and house-sat my apartment.

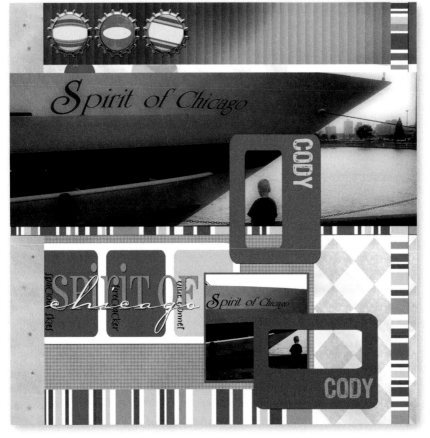

Washington D.C.

Amy Alvis, Indianapolis, Indiana

During her trip, Amy toured as much of Washington, D.C. as she could. She tightly cropped several photos of historic landmarks and combined them with larger pictures to create a photo border across the top of her page. She created her title by placing letter stickers over torn paper and tore the edges of her journaling block to match.

supplies: Cream, brown papers (Bazzill) • Letter stickers (Creative Imaginations) • Computer font

Spirit of Chicago

Tracey Lee, Dwight, Illinois

In this computer-generated layout, Tracy highlighted her son's fascination with this boat by framing him in a digital slide mount. The enlarged panoramic photo aptly convey's the boat's large size, especially in comparison to the small boy. Tracy repeated the rounded corners of the slide mounts within the title treatment for a sense of rhythm and repetition.

supplies: Image-editing software • Computer fonts

Pleasant Grove, Utah

Becky Thompson, Fruitland, Idaho

Becky used a crisp design to emphasize a dramtic photo. She created a striped border by combining patterned paper with orange and black papers. She framed a portion of patterned paper with the metal rim of a square tag and printed her quote directly on the white background.

supplies: White, orange, black papers (Bazzill) • Patterned paper (Design Originals) • Tag (Making Memories) • A & S Speedway, HP Sans fonts (fonts.com)

Las Vegas

Jennifer Bourgeault (Masters '04)

Jennifer documented a spontaneous trip to Las Vegas that she and her husband took with their friends. She accented her journaling with rhinestones and framed a journaling block with pictures from their trip. A ribbon finishes the page with a glitzy touch.

supplies: Red, white, black papers (Bazzill) • Rhinestones (Me & My Big Ideas) • Sticky Stitches ribbon (Colorbök) • Laser cut (Diecuts With a View) • Avant Garde font (myfonts.com)

When we tire of well-worn ways,
we seek for new.

This restless craving in the souls of men
spurs them to climb,

And to seek the *mountain view*.

-Ella Wheeler-Wilcox

Mountains outside of Pleasant Grove, UT – March 13, 2004

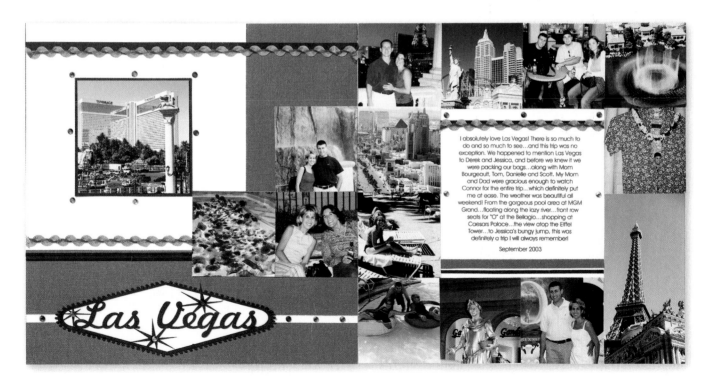

I absolutely love Las Vegas! There is so much to do and so much to see…and this trip was no exception. We happened to mention Las Vegas to Derek and Jessica, and before we knew it we were packing our bags…along with Mom Bourgeault, Tom, Danielle and Scott. My Mom and Dad were gracious enough to watch Connor for the entire trip…which definitely put me at ease. The weather was beautiful all weekend! From the gorgeous pool area at MGM Grand…floating along the lazy river…front row seats for "O" at the Bellagio…shopping at Caesars Palace…the view atop the Eiffel Tower…to Jessica's bungy jump, this was definitely a trip I will always remember!

September 2003

Mount Mitchell

Joanna Bolick (Masters '04)

Joanna and her husband took their son, Cole, for his first hike in the mountains of North Carolina. Patterned papers are a backdrop for an enlarged photo. Joanna placed a quote sticker on the photo to add to her journaling.

supplies: Blue paper • Patterned papers (Blue Cardigan, Basicgrey) • Quote stickers (Autumn Leaves) • Century Gothic font (fonts.com)

Pride of the Park

Becky Fleck, Columbus, Montana

With Yellowstone practically in her back yard, Becky and her family are able to visit many times throughout the year. Becky printed a map of the park on linen fabric and used it as the background. She aged some of the photos with sandpaper and walnut ink to give them rustic appeal. She used authentic feather and arrowhead accents to finish her page.

supplies: Cream paper • Graph patterned paper (KI Memories) • Gingham patterned paper (Daisy D's) • Blue patterned paper (Rusty Pickle) • Linen fabric (Jo-Ann) • Hemp cord • Date stamp, rub-ons (Making Memories) • Paige letter dies (Quickutz) • Twill tape • Walnut ink (7 Gypsies) • Arrowhead • Feathers • Glass, stone beads • Texas Hero font (fonts.com) • Butterbrotpapier font (1001fonts.com) • Austere Black font (downloaded from the Internet)

What I Will Miss

Sheila Doherty (Masters '05)

Forging ahead to a slower-paced life in a new state, Sheila recorded what she will miss about her family's life in California. She aged her background paper by crumpling, painting and inking the surface. She sanded the edges of several photos with sandpaper.

supplies: Purple, tan, ivory papers • Green patterned paper (Pebbles) • Transparency • Definition, leather photo corners, ribbon, photo turns, brads, alphabet stamps, metal letter, rub-ons (Making Memories) • Acrylic tag (Li'l Davis) • Address label, postmark, calendar (EK Success) • Label maker (Dymo) • Circle tag (Chatterbox) • Metal stencil • Jewelry tag • Stamping ink • Walnut ink • Alphabet stamps (Hero Arts) • Acrylic paint (Delta) • MaszynaAEG font (scrapbook-bytes.com) • The Hard Way, Malagua Demo fonts (dafont.com)

Deep and Wide

Rosemary Waits, Mustang, Oklahoma

Rosemary used the magnificence of the Grand Canyon as a metaphor for her family's love. Rosemary inked the edges of a map of the United States and placed it on green paper. She strategically placed the label holder over Arizona and the Grand Canyon region.

supplies: Blue, green papers (Bazzill) • Patterned paper (Design Originals) • Label holder • Brads • Stazon solvent ink (Tsukineko) • Photo corners

The Cottage

Elma Regnerus, Grimsby, Ontario, Canada

Elma had only a few pictures from her trip and although different in theme, collectively they told the story. Through the photos, journaling and title, she captures the laid-back fun of the cottage. Elma layered various papers on a rust background. She accented her title and photos with punched leaf shapes, some layered with vellum.

supplies: Rust, tan, green, blue papers (Scrapbook Sally) • Vellum • Ash leaf punch (Punch Bunch) • Square punch • Eyelets • Computer fonts

Kootenay National Park

Mary MacAskill, Alberta, Canada

Mary celebrated the Canadian Thanksgiving with a backpacking trip to the Fay Hut in Kootenay National Park. She put 15 photos on this page. It's a great trip summary. Mary cropped her photos in equal-size squares and tiled them across her patterned paper. She printed her title and journaling on a transparency and adhered it to her page.

supplies: Map • Transparency • Vellum • Dirty Deco font (highfonts.com) • Base 02 font (acidfonts.com)

Joshua Tree

Michele Rank, Cerritos, California

Michele double matted an enlarged photo on brown and green papers and then placed it on her background. She cropped photos into tags and hung them from buttons, which she placed on an accent strip over the main photo. Michele used a black pen to create a thin border around the edge of her patterned paper.

supplies: Brown, green and patterned papers, buttons, hemp, ink, pen, tag template and eyelets (Close to My Heart) • Computer font

Yosemite National Park

Hilary Erickson, Santa Clara, California

After a trip to Yosemite, Hilary and her family began to look forward to their move to California. Hilary printed her title and journaling on green paper and highlighted the edges with ink. She cropped several photos, placing them throughout her design, and anchored a journaling caption with an oversized brad.

supplies: Green paper (Bazzill) • Vellum (Chatterbox) • Computer fonts

My Yellowstone Days

Samantha Walker (Masters '05)

Samantha fondly remembers her summers at Yellowstone where her inspiration came from the art of God: nature. She aged the edges of her photo mats by roughing them with her fingernail and then applying ink. She placed her matted photos on textured paper and accented her design with inked fabric pieces. She used alphabet stamps on vellum to create a journaling accent and attached it to her picture with eyelets.

supplies: Light and dark brown, specialty papers (FLAX) • Vellum, alphabet stamps, brown ink (Stampin' Up) • Eyelets (Making Memories) • Fabric (Carole) • Computer fonts

Lake Tahoe Perspective

Deborah Liu
Santa Clara, California

In order to gain new perspective on a chaotic life, Deborah and her husband vacationed in peaceful Lake Tahoe. Deborah expanded her photo by cutting one side into strips to stretch across the page. She printed her journaling on a transparency and heat set the ink with embossing powder (see steps below). Deborah cut her title from yellow paper with a craft knife and accented her design with paper strips.

supplies: Blue, yellow, green papers (Bazzill) • Foam stamps (Making Memories) • Embossing powder • Embossing ink • Lainie Day font (dafont.com) • Stonehenge font (highfonts.com)

step by step

embossed column-format text

1. In a word-processing program, use sizing margins to format text into columns. For indenting, use Wrap function.

2. Print text onto a non-coated transparency using an inkjet printer.

3. Immediately after printing, sprinkle text with very fine embossing powder, tap off extra and heat. Do not burn the transparency—heat powder just until shiny.

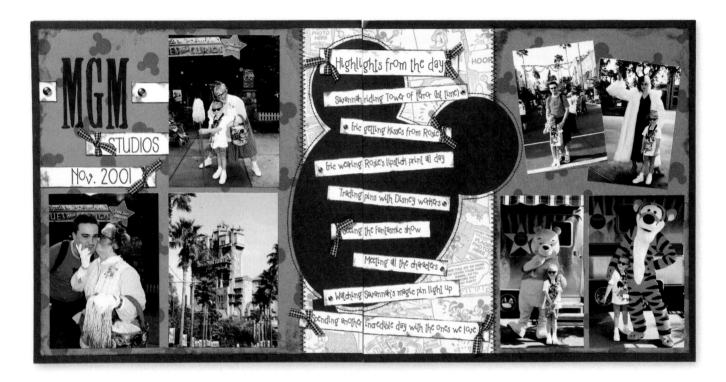

MGM Studios

Vanessa Hudson, Mount Olive, Alabama

Vanessa highlighted the events of her family trip to MGM Studios with bullet-style journaling. She first inked the edges of patterned paper and placed it on black paper, then stitched the two patterns together with a zigzag stitch. The journaling lies on top of the Mickey die cut, which she machine-stitched to the page.

supplies: Black paper (Bazzill) • Patterned paper (Sandylion) • Stamps (Making Memories) • Acrylic paint • Brads • Mickey die cut (Cut-It-Up) • Gingham ribbon

Magic Happens

Valerie Barton (Masters '03)

Valerie placed an enlarged photo over a gold border accented with a silhouette punch. She printed her journaling on vellum, tore the edges and embossed them with gold embossing powder. She then hid the journaling behind a hinged photo. She created her title using metal letters and letter stickers placed directly on her photo.

supplies: Black, red, patterned papers (Anna Griffin) • Embossed paper (K & Co.) • Letter stickers (EK Success) • Mickey punch (Plaid) • Stamp (Serendipity Stamps) • Frame (Card Connection) • Hinges • Computer fonts

Impishly You

Laurel Gervitz, Maple Grove, Minnesota

Just like Tigger, Laurel's daughter is playful and mischievous. Laurel inked the edges of her background paper and sanded them in various places. She stamped words on twill tape and hung tags from price tag holders, which she attached to the background with staples.

supplies: Black paper (Bazzill) • Patterned paper (Chatterbox) • Vellum (Worldwin) • Brads (Magic Scraps) • Letter stickers (Creative Imaginations, EK Success) • Twill tape (Creative Impressions) • Staples (Making Memories) • Alphabet stamps (Hero Arts, PSX) • Quote (Memories Complete) • Acrylic paint (Delta) • Price tag holders • Zig pen (EK Success)

Land of the Sun

Cherie Ward, Colorado Springs, Colorado

The large, dynamic shot on the left side is the centerpiece of the layout; it inspired the other shapes and accents. Cherie accented her layout with layered strips of paper along the bottom. She cut her title from blue and white papers and connected the double-page spread with sculpted metal strips.

supplies: Blue, purple, white papers (Bazzill) • Date rub-on (Autumn Leaves) • Metal accents (Making Memories) • Sonnets wax seal (Creative Imaginations) • Alphabet stamps (Hero Arts) • Transparency • Acrylic accent (KI Memories) • Barbarjowe font (dafont.com)

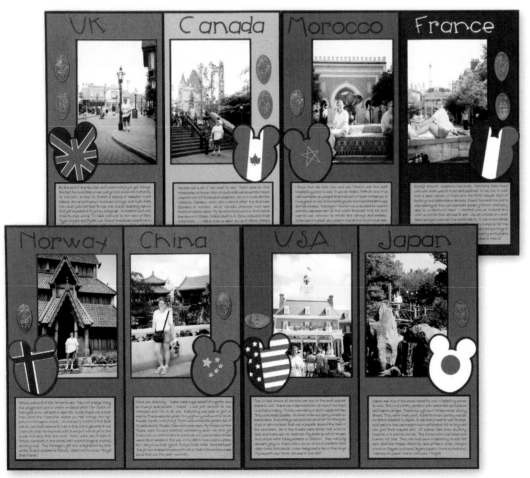

Epcot

Heidi Dillon
Salt Lake City, Utah

These layouts are from a vacation album Heidi created. Heidi's favorite part of Epcot was touring the world showcase. She divided her double-page layouts into quarters and used each to focus on a different country within the world showcase. She re-created each country's flag on a Mickey die cut. She also included pressed pennies that were collected throughout the tour.

supplies: Oatmeal, black, rust, mustard, green, navy, purple, white papers • Small, mini star punches • Maple leaf punch (Hyglo) • Mouse die cuts (Dayco) • Zig pen (EK Success) • Slick Writer pen (American Crafts) • Hemp • Computer font

Seuss Landing

Heidi Dillon, Salt Lake City, Utah

Everything about Seuss Landing made Heidi's family feel like they were in a Dr. Seuss book, she says. Heidi attached her photos to yellow paper using various colors of eyelets. She mounted the yellow paper on patterned paper and accented with slide-mount-framed photos. She used a photo of the park sign to create the page title.

supplies: Yellow, patterned papers (Club Scrap) • Eyelets (Doodlebug, Impress) • Slide mounts (Club Scrap) • Transparency (3M) • Computer font

Seeing Shamu

Julie Johnson (Master '05)

Seeing her son's face as Shamu jumped from the water for the first time made the hot crowded trip to Sea World worth it, Julie says. She cropped a photo into a mosaic, matted the individual blocks with black chipboard and pieced it back together. She printed her journaling on a transparency, painted the back with acrylic paint and adhered it with a spray adhesive.

supplies: Blue, white papers (Prism) • Chipboard (Bazzill) • Ribbon • Chipboard letters (Li'l Davis) • Charm letters (Making Memories) • Rub-ons (Making Memories) • Acrylic paint (Plaid) • Number stickers (Scrappy Cats) • Computer font

Splendor of the Sea

Donna Pittard, Kingwood, Texas

Donna's family enjoyed playing games and venturing out into the water during their visit to the beach. Donna stitched various papers to the background and embossed around the edges with clear extra thick embossing enamel. Throughout the page she incorporated sea-like texture with netting, shells and wave-inspiring fibers.

supplies: Tan, white, teal papers • Patterned paper (7 Gypsies) • Cheese cloth • Walnut ink • Fish stamp (Fred Mullet) • Glass beads (Blue Moon, Mill Hill) • Brads • Eyelets • Foofala die-cut letters (Autumn Leaves) • Ribbon • Fibers (Trendsetter Yarns) • Charm (Embellish It) • Skeletal leaves (Grafix) • Sculpey teal polymer clay (Polyform) • Wire • Ultra Thick Embossing Enamel (Ranger) • Sepia ink (Ranger) • Starfish • Seashell • Versamark (Tsukineko) • Cotton thread • Cézanne font (p22.com) • Dearest Swash font (myfonts.com) • Zothique Demo font (dafont.com)

Beach Memories

Danielle Layton, Clarksville, Tennessee

Danielle says, "Some people dream of the beach as a vacation, I think about it as home." She printed her photos, journaling and title on photo paper using image-editing software. She then added a patterned paper and ribbon border along the side.

supplies: White paper • Sara Lugg patterned paper (Paper Co.) • Ribbon (Making Memories) • Copperplate Gothic font (myfonts.com)

Beach…Horse…Heaven

Shelley Mclennan
St. Catharines, Ontario, Canada

Shelley mounted her photos from this horse-riding event on brown papers and placed them under and over her torn border. She layered various torn papers and vellum to create the background of her page. She cut her title from blue paper with a craft knife and accented a center border with eyelets and twine.

supplies: Teal, brown, tan papers • Patterned paper (Karen Foster) • Twine • Aladdin font (downloaded from the Internet)

Walk by the Ocean

Susan Weinroth, Philadelphia, Pennsylvania

Susan inked the edges of various patterned papers and layered them on brown and blue papers to create a clean, interconnected design. She accented her design with metal charms and ribbon. She created her title with rub-on letters and letter stickers with various ribbons tied at one corner.

supplies: Teal paper (Bazzill) • Patterned paper (SEI) • Letters (American Crafts) • Ribbon (Offray, May Arts, Li'l Davis) • Charms (Maude and Millie) • Stamping ink (Ranger) • Rub-ons (Making Memories) • Roxie font (twopeasinabucket.com)

Puerto Rico

Sandra Stephens, Woodbury, Minnesota

Sandra layered patterned paper on brown and blue papers. She mounted her photo on blue satin and accented a premade tag with photos, ribbon and label tape. She used foam stamps and acrylic paint to create her title.

supplies: Blue, brown papers (Bazzill) • Sand patterned paper (Cloud 9) • Palm tree patterned paper (American Traditional) • Fabric (Jo-Ann) • Mesh ribbon (Offray) • Green ribbon (SEI) • Canvas tags (Creative Imaginations) • Square tag (Making Memories) • Foam alphabet stamps (Making Memories) • Acrylic paint (Plaid) • Label maker (Dymo) • Computer font

Beach Baby

Janice Carson, Hamilton, Ontario, Canada

Janice's photo shoot with her son at the beach allowed him time to play in the water while she enjoyed a favorite hobby—photography. Janice placed textured paper on a cream background and then layered various photos. She cut her title from black paper with a craft knife and accented her layout with an embroidered sun.

supplies: Cream, blue, black papers (Bazzill) • Blue textured paper • Alphabet stamps (PSX) • Stamping ink • Sun accent (Manuela) • Blackjack font (1001fonts.com) • Papyrus font (linotype.com)

Saltwater Euphoria

Michelle Pendleton
Colorado Springs, Colorado

Michelle's experience at the beach with her daughter and the smell of saltwater was nothing short of euphoric, as captured on this page. Michelle layered various shades of teal papers to create the background and framed her design with beads strung through embroidery floss. She extended her photo onto an original frame (see steps below) as well as on her background paper.

supplies: Teal papers • Pigment ink (Clearsnap) • Watermark ink (Tsukineko) • Embossing ink (Clearsnap) • Shrink plastic • Beads (Stampendous, Cousin Crop) • Wire • Cheesecloth • Modeling paste (Liquitex) • Acrylic paint • Tulle • Twine • Lettering templates (Crafter's Workshop) • Stazon solvent ink (Tsukineko) • Alphabet stamps (Making Memories) • Thread • Mod Podge (Plaid) • Phrase stamp (Hero Arts) • Silver embroidery floss (DMC) • Transparency (3M) • Micro eyelets (Creative Impressions) • Ultra Thick Embossing Enamel (Ranger) • Nick Bantock stamping ink (Ranger) • Foam adhesive • Zig pen (EK Success) • Sea Gull charm (Embellish It) • Chipboard • Typist, Modern No. 20 fonts (downloaded from the Internet) • Watson font (Chatterbox) • Palatino Linotype font (myfonts.com)

step by step

sea-inspired frame

1. Using photo, create a guide to cut frame from chipboard. Mark water and horizon lines on guide to match photo.

2. Apply thin layer of modeling paste on frame. Apply tulle to top of frame (sky), add more paste to secure and let dry.

3. Apply paste to bottom of frame, add cheesecloth (water). Build up surf area with fiber strips and paste. Let dry.

4. Paint frame in colors to coordinate with photo.

Jungle Green

Pamela James, Ventura, California

Pamela says trekking through the jungle was like "opening a box of crayons and pulling out every shade of green." She layered green papers and tore patterned papers to create the mat for her photos. She altered the color of gold skeleton leaves with green ink and enhanced the page with a multimedia, textural title treatment.

supplies: Light and dark green papers (Bazzill) • Patterned paper (Provo Craft) • Vellum (Worldwin) • Letter squares (Hot Off the Press) • Skeleton leaves • Beads • Wire • Metal plaque (Making Memories) • Eyelets • Papyrus font (linotype.com) Shoshoni Brush font (downloaded from the Internet)

Barefoot in San Pedro

Sandra Stephens, Woodbury, Minnesota

Sandra lavished this page with wonderful photos that truly capture the mood of this festive locale. Sandra placed an enlarged photo on yellow paper and accented the layout with strips of raspberry paper. She heat embossed paper strips to add texture to them. She cut her title from raspberry and yellow papers.

supplies: Blue, yellow, raspberry papers (Bazzill) • Versamark watermark ink (Tsukineko) • Embossing powder (Judikins) • Computer fonts

Majestic Mexican Vacation

Samantha Walker (Masters '05)

Samantha created the look of stucco on her paper using a chunky paintbrush to build up several layers of gesso. She then painted a brick background on watercolor paper and adhered it behind torn portions of her paper. The tile frame around her photo was created by printing a tile design on paper and then applying five layers of embossing powder. (see steps below)

supplies: Watercolor paper (Fabriano) • White mat board • Vellum • Gesso (Grumbacher) • Watercolor, acrylic paints (Winsor Newton) • Label holder (Jo-Ann) • Stamp, ink, fiber, embossing powder (Stampin' Up) • Chipboard • Ultra Thick Embossing Enamel (Ranger) • Alphabet stamps (Hero Arts) • Tile design (tierrayfuego.com)

step by step

Mexican tile frame

1. Select and print multiple copies of tile design from Web site (see supply list). Cut into 1" squares.

2. Cut 1" squares of chipboard and adhere tile designs to squares.

3. Heat emboss with several layers of extra thick embossing enamel.

4. Combine gesso and burnt sienna paint for "grout" with palette knife and rub onto frame. Press tiles into frame.

Our Travels,
Our Honeymoon

Laurel Gervitz, Maple Grove, Minnesota

Laurel created mini travel journals for each of her honeymoon destinations. At the top of her layout she placed a wall of photos. On the bottom, Laurel created a collaged background using patterned paper, corrugated paper, tags, ribbon and ephemera. She embellished the front of each journal and accented them with ribbons.

supplies: Black paper (Bazzill) • Patterned paper (Rusty Pickle) • Patterned transparencies (Li'l Davis, 7 Gypsies) • Walnut ink, tissue paper, square buckles, metal loops, alligator clasp (7 Gypsies) • Spiral clips (Making Memories) • Sticker (Me & My Big Ideas) • Stamping ink (Ranger) • Metal letters (Colorbök) • Journal books (DMD) • Computer font

Italy

Joanne MacIntyre, Medford, New York

Joanne's title page for her album about a trip to Italy includes a glimpse of each city she toured. She layered each picture on various colors of paper and offset gray matting for a shadowed effect. She printed the city name on vellum and attached it to the top of each picture.

supplies: Blue, rust, gray, brown, tan, green papers • Vellum • Chalk • Stickers (Frances Meyers, Mrs. Grossman's, Creative Memories) • Stamps • Computer fonts

High Tide at Venice

Joanne MacIntyre, Medford, New York

Joanne saw that high tide in Venice meant that water from the Grand Canal came directly onto the walkway as seen in the photos. She layered various papers treated with chalk, ink and paint to create a stained glass background. She matted an enlarged photo on black paper and placed it on the bottom portion of her page.

supplies: Black, white papers (Bazzill) • Vellum • Chalk • Stamping Ink (Ranger) • Pigment ink (Tsukineko) • Acrylic paint, date stamp (Making Memories) • Santa's Sleigh, CBX Trumpet fonts (downloaded from the Internet)

Oberammergau

Joanne MacIntyre, Medford, New York

Joanne silhouette cut each building from her photos and matted them on green paper, which she layered on patterned paper. She used tree stickers to disguise the edge of the buildings. Her title is handcut from green paper with a craft knife.

supplies: Green papers (Bazzill) • Patterned paper (Provo Craft) • Ribbon, flowers, alphabet stamps (Making Memories) • Mesh (Magic Mesh) • Buttons • Fern punch • Charm • Computer fonts

Prague

Danielle Thompson, Tucker, Georgia

Danielle layered several patterned papers and machine stitched them together with black thread. She covered some photos with a film-strip transparency and enclosed her journaling in an embellished envelope.

supplies: Patterned papers (Design Originals, Creative Imaginations, Rusty Pickle, Autumn Leaves, PSX) • Quote sticker (Colorbök) • Postage stamp sticker (K & Co.) • Envelope • Beads • Ribbon • All Night Media heart stamp (Plaid) • Clip (EK Success) • Flowers (Prima) • Karen Russell filmstrip (Creative Imaginations) • Alphabet stamps (Hero Arts) • Photo corners (Making Memories) • Tag • Twill tape

Croatia

Danielle Thompson, Tucker, Georgia

Danielle used an enlarged photo as the background of her design placing patterned papers along the top. She framed various photos with letter stickers cut in half and accented with photo corners, circle clips and a woven label.

supplies: Gold, olive papers (Bazzill) • Patterned papers (Paper Loft, 7 Gypsies, Anna Griffin, PSX, K & Co.) • Ribbon (Offray, Michaels) • Label holder, metal letters (Making Memories) • Buckle letters (Basicgrey, Paper Loft) • Photo corners (EK Success, Pioneer) • Threads woven label (Me & My Big Ideas) • Clips (Boxer) • File folder (Autumn Leaves)

Remembering Paris

Kara Wylie, Frisco, Texas

On this page, Kara listed reasons why she fell in love with Paris. She tore and inked the edges of brown patterned paper and machine stitched it to cream paper. She accented several photos with folded strips of ribbon, which she attached with staples.

supplies: Blue, brown papers • Patterned papers (K & Co., American Traditional) • Ribbons (Me & My Big Ideas, Li'l Davis) • Label maker (Dymo) • Index tabs • Brads • Stamping ink (Clearsnap) • Computer fonts

Paris, I Love You

Michelle Mueller, Albion, Michigan

While enjoying ice cream at a café, Michelle watched the scenes shown in her photos unfold before her. Michelle embellished one photo and created coordinating accents using orange embossed papers. She framed two photos with orange paper and adhered them to embellished patterned paper. She created her title by printing on a transparency and with rub-ons.

supplies: Blue, patterned papers, stamping ink, stamp (Club Scrap) • Transparencies (Artchix, 7 Gypsies, Library Layers) • Frame (Nunn) • Ribbons (Stampendous, Boxer, Lavish Lines) • Acrylic paint (Plaid) • Ultra Thick Embossing Enamel (Ranger) • Computer font

Carrick-A-Rhede

Meryl Bartho, Pinetown, KwaZulu, South Africa

The fact that Meryl was short on photos for this layout forced her to be more creative, she says. She enlarged three dramatic shots to show the beautiful landscapes. She also cropped images from the photos to create digital accents for this computer-generated page.

supplies: Photoshop Creative Suite image-editing software (Adobe) • Digital scrapbooking kit (designed by Meryl, available at digitalscrapbookplace.com)

Watercolor Palette

Madeline Fox, River Ridge, Louisiana

An overcast day and light sea mist made the coast of Italy appear to have been painted with watercolors. Madeline capitalized on that look for her layout. She placed her photo on patterned paper and sanded the edges. She adhered various strips of lace to her background and placed her picture on top.

supplies: Patterned papers (Karen Foster, Provo Craft) • Vellum • All Night Media embossing stencil (Plaid) • Fibers (Fibers by the Yard) • Metallic rub-ons (Craf-T) • Alphabet brads (Scrap Essentials) • Lace (Jo-Ann) • Flower • Button • Vellum tag (Jo-Ann)

Westminster Abbey

Sheryl Highsmith
Fort Collins, Colorado

Westminster Abbey architecture is so impressive that Sheryl placed a wall of photos along the top of her page. Her journaling and title were printed on paper. She also accented the title with stencil letters.

supplies: Sedona papers (Bazzill) • Stencil letters (Office Depot) • Acrylic paint (Plaid) • Embroidery floss (DMC) • Charm • Nailheads • Copper frame (Nunn) • London cutout (K & Co.) • Rub-on letters (Chatterbox) • Computer fonts

Reykjavik

Sheryl Highsmith
Fort Collins, Colorado

Sheryl placed several photos close together on red paper and accented with yellow paper strips. She printed her journaling on yellow paper and created her title with chipboard letters.

supplies: Red, yellow papers (Bazzill) • Chipboard letters (Li'l Davis)

Right in the middle of busy Tokyo I was happy to find places of solitude, peace and harmony. Here, the children and I would enjoy a picnic lunch and the beautiful scenery. All through Japan there is a common mix of the very modern with the very old and traditional.
It is a very comforting mix.

Tokyo 1984

Harmony

Andrea Vetten-Marley (Masters '04)

In the middle of a hectic city, Andrea found a place of solitude as well as to enjoy picnics with her children. She placed teal paper on black paper and machine stitched around the edges. Using a template as a guide, she hand stitched a bamboo shoot with black embroidery floss. She heat embossed her title for shine and dimension.

supplies: Teal, black papers (Bazzill) • Patterned paper • Asian coins • Alphabet, signature stamps (Club Scrap) • Bamboo template (Plaid) • Embroidery floss (DMC) • Versamark watermark ink (Tsukineko) • Embossing powder • Thread

The Photos I Don't Have

Emma Finlay, Dublin, Ireland

Emma's hunt for wild predators may not have worked as she'd planned, but now she has a funny story to tell on this page. She printed her journaling on orange paper and layered it with a darker shade. She used a postcard to create the title and accented her page with animal charms.

supplies: Orange papers • Charms (Embellish It) • Computer font • Bog Standard font (dafont.com)

The Big Five
SOUTH AFRICA

This is a page about the photos I don't have.

All the books I had read talked of the big five, all the parks sold themselves on how many they had, all the postcards reinforced the message. You want to see these five animals. And yes we saw two but they're frankly the most boring pair. Rhinos are pretty cool and Hluhluwe has lots and is very interesting about them. But buffaloes are basically angry cows. The guides and books talk about how fierce and dangerous they are but they're just not all that exciting. Every wildlife program I've seen and book I've read make me want to see the cats and the elephants. Adam and Laura did see elephants in a different park before I came but the only predators we ever saw were small spotted genets and a single hyena. We were so eager to find them we were spotting animals where there were none and that's how we saw.....

The lion that was an antelope.

At dawn on the third day we had got up really early to get to the park again and were now sitting on a little dirt track off the main road, up a hill among the bushes and thorn trees. I had finished taking sunrise pictures when Adam caught some movement in the bushes that could be the flicker of an ear. He said it was a lion and we all got so excited and considered it a reward for being up so early. Laura thought she had seen something and I was bouncing around the car peering through the thorns in the grey light asking where and furious that I was missing it. Adam moved the car and climbed right out the window, standing so only his lower legs were still inside. The animal moved again and we could see the head and shoulders of ...an antelope. A new kind we hadn't seen before but no majestic predator.

The elephant that was a buffalo.

After a very rushed changing of a punctured tyre we had set out on our morning walk with an armed guard who had started by cautioning us to be quiet, to stop immediately if told to and to run fast if needed. It was wonderful to be out walking in an African dawn and surrounded by giraffes looking down on us from the tree tops. The guide would stop and point out various interesting things and one was a pile of elephant dung. It looked pretty fresh and there was more as we walked back towards a dry riverbed near the car. We were coming down towards it when he suddenly stopped, made us all back up quickly and led us behind some bushes to get upstream. There were noises of something large in the bushes down at the river bed and I was now utterly convinced we had been stalking an elephant and were about to see a wild, enormous elephant. We came quietly down into the river bed and looked down to see.. a buffalo peacefully having breakfast.

The leopard that was a log.

At least the others were really animals! We had agreed that it's better to go back 20 times for false alarms than to miss something good. I did say from the start that it probably wasn't anything but I made Adam back up a bit and squinted across the clearing and zoomed my camera and managed to persuade myself it really was a leopard! I wanted so badly to be the one to find a cat. I got all excited and woke Laura to get her hopes up too but finally had to admit it was a dark branch lying behind the yellow grass with the stump of a branch sticking up for an ear.

closed

Japan

Tricia Rubens
Castle Rock, Colorado

Tricia created a hinged layout, that when opened, reveals the treasures of her trip to Japan (see opened layout below). To create each layout "door," she cut an additional piece of black paper in half and attached it to her layout with black hinges. Tricia embellished each door with photos, slide mounts, memorabilia and accents.

supplies: Patterned papers (7 Gypsies) • Silkscreen paper • Letter stickers (Wordsworth) • Scrappy Chic accent stickers (Me & My Big Ideas) • Nostalgiques accent stickers (EK Success) • Sonnets wax seal (Creative Imaginations) • Tags (Limited Edition) • Metal Chinese keys • Stamps, frame, safety pins (Making Memories) • Alphabet stamps (Wordsworth, Hero Arts) • Walnut ink • Pigment ink (Tsukineko) • Acrylic paint (Plaid) • Slide holder (Magic Scraps) • Label holder (Li'l Davis) • Metal clip (7 Gypsies)

open

The Ancient City of

K y o t o

1. Heian Jingu Shrine, an ancient Shinto Japanese court
2. Entrance sign explains the history of the Heian Shrine
3. Label from gilded silk screened Japanese paper
4. Dragon fountain of the three tiered Kiyomizu Temple
5. Japanese ponds and gardens of the Heian Shrine
6. Ancient Buddha statue of the Kiyomizu Temple
7. Dragon fountain located in the courtyard, Heian Shrine
8. Ancient lane with pottery stores leading to Kiyomizu
9. Temple building with brightly colored paint, Kiyomizu

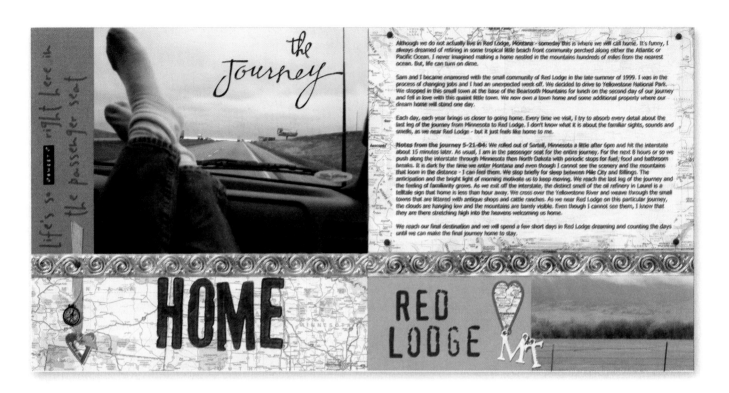

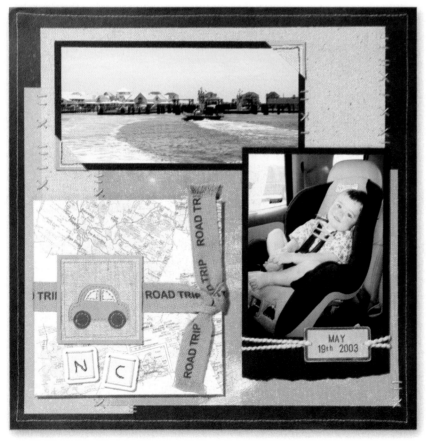

The Journey Home

Jodi Heinen (Masters '05)

Jodi advocates journaling on the road to capture the memories. Much of the journaling on this page came straight from her travel journal. Jodi used portions of a road map for her patterned paper. She painted a whitewash over the paper and once dry used it to print her journaling. She accented with metal strips and placed rub-on letters directly on her photo.

supplies: Gray paper • Map paper (from atlas) • Acrylic paint • Label maker (Dymo) • Heart charm • Ribbon • Metal letters, foam stamps, metal molding, brads (Making Memories) • Brads • Hootie font (momscorner4kids.com) • Tahoma font (myfonts.com) • Cookie Dough font (twopeasinabucket.com)

Road Trip

Cindy Smith, Knoxville, Tennessee

Cindy's son enjoyed the view from his car seat during their trip to North Carolina, as shown in this photo. Cindy layered patterned paper on her background and accented it with handstitching. She included additional photos and journaling in a book attached to her page. To create the title, she printed on twill tape.

supplies: Black paper (Bazzill) • Patterned paper, tiles, sticker, car die cut (Sweetwater) • Date stamp • Twill • String

Is Y'all Really a Word?

Nic Howard (Masters '05)

Nic became fascinated with the expression "y'all" when traveling to the United States. She used her surprise at its existence to theme her page about her first solo overseas trip. She accented her design with a ribbon border and embellished the title with clear gloss medium.

supplies: Light and dark blue papers (Bazzill) • Patterned paper (7 Gypsies) • Alphabet stamps (PSX) • Rubber stamp (Oxford Impressions) • Stamping Ink • Ribbon (Making Memories) • Aleene's Paper Glaze clear gloss medium (Duncan) • Georgia font (myfonts.com)

Going Home

Sheila Doherty (Masters '05)

Sheila braved a long trip alone with her three children under the age of 4, which she documented on this page. She inked the edges of various patterned papers and layered them on a blue background.

supplies: Blue, brown, pink papers (Bazzill) • Patterned papers (Design Originals, Autumn Leaves, KI Memories) • Rub-on letters (KI Memories) • Ribbon (Michaels) • Brads • Stamping ink • Stazon solvent ink (Tsukineko) • Alphabet stamps (Hero Arts) • Acrylic paint (Delta) • Clock (7 Gypsies)

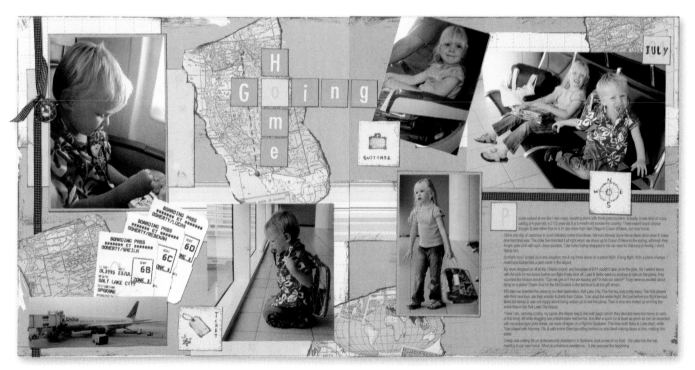

product guide

The following companies manufacture the products featured in this book.
Check your local scrapbook retailer or arts-and-crafts store to find the products.

3L, Ltd.
800-828-3130 3LCorp.com

3M Stationery
800-364-3577 3m.com

7 Gypsies
323-725-1975 7gypsies.com

Accent Factory
accentfactory.com

AccuCut®
800-288-1670 accucut.com
(wholesale only)

Adobe™
adobe.com

All My Memories
888-553-1998 allmymemories.com

American Crafts
800-879-5185 americancrafts.com
(wholesale only)

American Tag Company
800-223-3956 americantag.net

American Traditional™ Designs
800-448-6656 americantraditional.com

Anna Griffin, Inc.
888-817-8170 annagriffin.com
(wholesale only)

Artchix Studios
artchixstudio.com

Autumn Leaves
800-588-6707

Avery® Dennison
averydennison.com

BasicGrey
basicgrey.com

Bazzill Basics Paper
480-558-8557 bazzillbasics.com

Beadery, The
thebeadery.com

Beads & Plenty More
519-47-BEADS
beadsandplentymore.com

Blue Cardigan Designs
bluecardigan.com

Blue Moon Beads
800-377-6715 beads.net

Bobbin Ribbon
800-466-7393 morexcorp.com

Boxer Scrapbook Productions
503-625-0455 boxerscrapbooks.com

Card Connection, The
cardconnection.com

Caren's Crafts
scrapbooking4fun.com

Carole Fabrics
carolefabrics.com

Chatterbox, Inc.
208-939-9133 chatterboxinc.com

C-Line Products
c-line.com

Clearsnap®, Inc.
800-448-4862 clearsnap.com
(wholesale only)

Close To My Heart
888-655-6552 closetomyheart.com

Cloud 9 Design™
763-493-0990
cloud9design.biz

Club Scrap™, Inc.
888-634-9100 clubscrap.com

Coats & Clark
800-648-1479 coatsandclark.com

Colorbök™, Inc.
800-366-4660 colorbok.com
(wholesale only)

Costco
costco.com

Cousin Corp. of America
727-536-3568 cousin.com

Craf-T Products
507-236-3996 craftproducts.com

Crafter's Workshop, The
877-CRAFTER
thecraftersworkshop.com

Creating Keepsakes
creatingkeepsakes.com

Creative Imaginations
800-942-6487 cigift.com
(wholesale only)

Creative Impressions
719-596-4860
creativeimpressions.com

Creative Memories
800-468-9335 creative-memories.com

Creative Paperclay
800-899-5952 paperclay.com

C-Thru® Ruler Company, The
800-243-8419 cthruruler.com
(wholesale only)

Cut-it-up
cut-it-up.com

Daisy D's Paper Company
888-601-8955 daisydspaper.com

Delta Technical Coatings, Inc.
800-423-4135 deltacrafts.com

Deluxe Designs™
480-497-9005 deluxecuts.com

Demis Products, Inc.
demisproducts.com

Design Originals
800-877-7820 d-originals.com

Destination Stickers and Stamps
866-806-7826 destinationstickers.com

Die Cuts With a View™
801-224-6766 diecutswithaview.com

DMC Corporation
973-589-0606 dmc-usa.com

DMD Industries, Inc.
800-805-9890 dmdind.com
(wholesale only)

Doodlebug Design™
801-966-9952 timelessmemories.ca

Dritz
dritz.com (wholesale only)

Duncan Enterprises
800-438-6226
duncan-enterprises.com

Dymo
dymo.com

Eastman Kodak Company
770-522-2542 kodak.com

EK Success™, Ltd.
800-524-1349 eksuccess.com
(wholesale only)

Emagination Crafts, Inc.
630-833-9521 emaginationcrafts.com
(wholesale only)

Embellish It
720-312-1628 embellishit.com

Embossing Arts Company
541-928-9898 embossingarts.com

Fabriano
cartierefabriano.it

Far and Away
farandawayscrapbooks.com

Fiber Scraps
215-230-4905 fiberscraps.com

Fibers By The Yard
800-760-8901 fibersbytheyard.com

Flair Designs
888-546-9990 flairdesignsinc.com

FLAX Art & Design
flaxart.com

Foofala
402-330-3208 foofala.com

Frances Meyer®, Inc.
800-372-6237 francesmeyer.com

Freckle Press
frecklepress.com

Fred Mullet
fredbmullet.com

Fuji
fujifilm.com

Glue Dots International
888-688-7131 gluedots.com

Go West Studios
goweststudios.com

Grumbacher
grumbacherart.com

Hammermill
hammermill.com

Hampton Art, LLC
800-229-1019 hamptonart.com
(wholesale only)

Happy Hammer, The
303-690-3883
thehappyhammer.com

Hero Arts® Rubber Stamps, Inc.
800-822-4376 heroarts.com
(wholesale only)

Hobby Lobby
hobbylobby.com

Hot Off The Press, Inc.
800-227-9595 craftpizazz.com

Hyglo
hyglocrafts.com

Hyman Hendler and Sons
hymanhendler.com

IBM
ibm.com

Impress Rubber Stamps
206-901-9101
impressrubberstamps.com

Inkadinkado® Rubber Stamps
800-888-4652 inkadinkado.com

Jo-Ann Fabrics
joannfabrics.com

JudiKins
310-515-5115 judikins.com

Junkitz
junkitz.com

K & Company
888-244-2083 kandcompany.com

Karen Foster Design™
801-451-9779 karenfosterdesign.com
(wholesale only)

KI Memories
972-243-5595 kimemories.com

Kolo®, LLC
800-636-5656 kolo.com

Krylon
800-4KRYLON

Lasting Impressions for Paper, Inc.
800-9-EMBOSS

Lavish Lines
lavishlines.com

Leave Memories
leavememories.com

Li'l Davis Designs
949-838-0344 lildavisdesigns.com

Limited Edition Rubber Stamps
650-594-4242 LimitedEditionRS.com

Liquitex®
888-4ACRYLIC liquitex.com

Magic Mesh™
magicmesh.com

Magic Scraps™
972-238-1838
magicscraps.com

Making Memories
800-286-5263
makingmemories.com

Marvy® Uchida
800-541-5877 uchida.com
(wholesale only)

Maude and Millie
maudeandmillie.com

Me & My Big Ideas
949-583-2065
meandmybigideas.com
(wholesale only)

Memories Complete
866-966-6365
memoriescomplete.com

Michaels® Arts & Crafts
800-642-4235 michaels.com

Microsoft
microsoft.com

Mill Hill Beads
millhillbeads.com

Mrs. Grossman's
mrsgrossmans.com

Mustard Moon™ Paper Co.
408-229-8542 mustardmoon.com

My Sentiments Exactly!
sentiments.com

Nunn Design
nunndesign.com

Office Depot
officedepot.com

OfficeMax
officemax.com

Offray & Son, Inc.
offray.com

Oxford Impressions
oxfordimpressions.com

Paper Company, The
800-426-8989 thepaperco.com

Paper Loft, The
801-254-1961 paperloft.com
(wholesale only)

Paper Love Designs
paperlovedesigns.com

Pebbles, Inc.
pebblesinc.com

PhotoPOSTOS
photopostos.com

Pioneer Photo Albums
800-366-3686
pioneerphotoalbums.com

Plaid Enterprises, Inc.
800-842-4197 plaidonline.com

Polaroid Corp.
polaroid.com (wholesale only)

Prima Marketing, Inc.
primamarketinginc.com

Prism
prismpapers.com

Provo Craft®
888-577-3545 provocraft.com
(wholesale only)

PSX Design™
800-782-6748 psxdesign.com

Punch Bunch
254-791-4209 punchbunch.com

Pulsar Paper Products
pulsarpaper.com

QuickKutz®
888-702-1146 quickkutz.com

Rand McNally
randmcnally.com

Ranger Industries, Inc.
800-244-2211 rangerink.com

Reminiscence Papers
reminiscencepapers.com

River City Rubber Works
877-735-BARN
rivercityrubberworks.com

Rubber Stampede
800-423-4135 rubberstampede.com

Rusty Pickle, The
801-274-9588 rustypickle.com

Sam Flax
samflax.com

Sandylion Sticker Designs
800-387-4215 sandylion.com

Scrap Arts
501-631-4893 scraparts.com

Scrapbook Sally
866-SBSALLY scrapbooksally.com

Scrappy Cat, LLC
440-234-4850
scrappycatcreations.com

Scrapworks, LLC
scrapworks.com

Scrapyard 329
775-829-1118 scrapyard329.com

Sculpey
sculpey.com

SEI, Inc.
800-333-3279 shopsei.com

Serendipity Stamps
816-532-0740 serendipitystamps.com

Sony
sony.com

Stampabilities
800-888-0321 stampabilities.com

Stampendous!®
800-869-0474 stampendous.com

Stampin' Up!®
800-782-6787 stampinup.com

Stewart Superior
800-558-2875 stewartsuperior.com

Sticker Studio™
stickerstudio.com

Sulyn Industries
sulyn.com

Sweetwater Scrapbook Stickers & Papers
800-359-3094
sweetwaterscrapbooks.com

Therm O Web, Inc.
800-323-0799 thermoweb.com
(wholesale only)

Trendsetter Yarns
trendsetteryarns.com

Tsukineko®, Inc.
800-769-6633 tsukineko.com

USArtQuest
800-200-7848 usartquest.com

Wal-Mart
walmart.com

Weavewerks
weavewerks.com

Winsor & Newton
winsornewton.com

Wordsworth Stamps
719-282-3495
wordsworthstamps.com

WorldWin Extraordinary Papers
888-843-6455 worldwinpapers.com

Wrights® Ribbon Accents
877-597-4448

We have made every attempt to properly credit the items mentioned in this book. If any company has been listed incorrectly, please contact Darlene D'Agostino at darlene.dagostino@fwpubs.com.